Swing Trading 101

Discover the Best Strategies, Tools, and Tactics to Become a Successful Trader

By Trevis White

Table of Contents

Introduction

Congratulations on purchasing this book and thank you for doing so.

The world of trading is growing increasingly chaotic. Purchasing this book is the first step that you can take towards doing something about your financial situation. The first step will not always be the easiest, which is why the information you will find in the following chapters is essential, as they are not concepts that can be put into action immediately. If you file these concepts away for when you need them, when the time comes to actually use them, you will be glad you have them at hand.

The following chapters will discuss the primary preparedness principles that you will need to consider if you ever hope to really make money swing trading. This means that you will want to consider the quality of your entry and stop loss, including the potential issues raised by their ratio, how they can best be utilized in a strategy, as well as various tools you might need to keep your mind focused on the task at hand.

With those out of the way, you will then learn everything you need to know about money management. Rounding out the three primary requirements for successful swing trading, you will then learn about crucial techniques that will help you on your journey.

I am happy to welcome you to the world of swing trading and to help you make more money.

Chapter 1

Getting Started with Swing Trading

In this book, we will show you all the steps you need to take to invest in forex from home. We will show you how to play on the forex market, how to choose the best pairs to invest in, but above all, how to invest in forex and currencies.

In addition, we will also mention the possible methods to invest in online forex exchanges, thanks to online trading. All the concepts that you will find in this guide have been written to be also understood by people unrelated to the world of online trading and the stock exchange, that is, those who have decided to inquire to start investing in the stock market.

Investing in the forex market means buying and selling currencies, aiming to earn between the price difference (purchase and sale). In the world of the forex exchange, as in other major financial markets (for example, stock market and CFD), you can earn both when there is an increase in the value of a stock and when there is a fall in the value of a stock.

Today, thanks to online trading, it is possible to invest in forex simply from home without problems. This is possible, thanks to online trading platforms better known as brokers.

Today, it is possible to invest in the forex exchange mainly through the following methods:

- forex market
- binary options trading
- CFD trading (contract for difference)

In this case, you can choose one of the following online, regulated, and authorized trading platforms shown below:

1. Markets.com

2. 24Option.com

3. iqoption.com

4. BDSwiss.com

In short, with online trading, everyone can start making money on the forex market. It does not matter whether you are a novice trader or an experienced trader. Online trading is offered to everyone, thanks to the training offered by its broker, which teaches the basics of trading. Moreover, many brokers today allow you to practice with a demo account, thanks to which all traders can test not only the trading platform, but they can start experimenting with their trading strategies and take their first steps in this fantastic world.

Very often, the concepts of saving and investing are confused, as well as that of "saver" and "trader." However, there are substantial differences that need to be understood before diving deeper into the subject of money.

In this chapter, we will explain what saving and investing are, analyzing which choice is more convenient today.

Saving means taking out a portion of income received, that you deliberately choose not to consume immediately, but to store in a bank account for the future. Saving often results in the tranquility guaranteed by the availability of resources to deal with unexpected situations.

Savings can then be allocated to investment, and this is the main analogy between the two concepts. The investment may be of the "economic" type (such as the purchase of a car or company machinery) or of the "financial" type (such as the purchase of a security or mutual fund with the objective to see capital growth over time). However, unlike savings, in the case of investing, the achievement of the desired objective is not certain (for example, a stock may lose value), so the result can be negative, compromising the amounts saved.

Which is better?

If the question that arises is whether it is better to save or invest, the answer is probably "both." The choice depends on your financial situation and your personal goals.

Savings can be used to invest, but can also be used in other ways. In fact, the money saved can also be deposited in the bank to reduce risks (theft). But this, unlike what many think, is a wrong and unprofitable choice. Money, in fact, tends to lose purchasing power over time due to inflation. In other words, if you save $100 today, in 20 years, you will be able to get less out of that money than today. This is why saving money is often the wrong choice if you want to get wealthy.

Assuming an average increase in the cost of living around 2% and a saved sum of $5,000, in five years, this sum will fall to real $4,500. That is 10% less (excluding banking taxes!). Obviously, you can keep the savings at home (under the classic mattress!), but with all the risks that come with it.

What is the Difference between Trading and Saving?

Let's repeat it once again to get it better. Saving means to put money aside little by little in order to accumulate a certain sum. Usually, you save for a certain goal, like going on vacation, buying a car, or for emergencies that could happen.

Instead, trading means taking a part of the money to make it grow, buying tools that can increase its value like currencies, real estates, and ETF's.

Who should save?

Obviously, everyone should try to save a part of their money. The rule is to have away on your bank account at least the necessary to "survive" for three months and cover the main expenses (such as food and rent). This will offer air pocket, in case of inconvenient and unexpected situations.

Saving is, therefore, a rule and as every good rule, it has its exceptions. You can, in fact, stop putting aside the money when:

- You have too much debt, and you are trying to pay it off
- The family has priority and could not go on in case of unfortunate events to one of its members.

Even when you have set aside enough for emergencies, you do not have to stop saving. The goal of everyone should be to put aside at least 10% of their salary every month, perhaps starting from 5% and gradually scaling up. To make things easier, you can save money by thinking of any objective, like having enough money for a great honeymoon or to get a new car.

Having a goal is essential, so you know what you're saving up for. Every rich person has financial goals, so it is a good habit to pick up.

When is it the time to trade?

Like when you save money, you need to have a goal to when and how to trade your savings. In this case, it is important to know what your short, medium, and long-term goals are.

- With "short term," we mean goals for the next 3 years
- With "medium term," things are planned for the next 3-10 years
- The "long-term" goals are those for which you will not need the money back for at least 10 years or more

For short-term objectives, you usually invest through deposit accounts, which allow you to get a minimum return in a short amount of time. However, this has been a bit shrinking in the last period (deposit rates are at the lowest). For the medium-long term objectives, it is instead advisable to invest in the market, to avoid the reduction in value that inflation produces on "still" money. The market guarantees usually higher returns than deposit accounts over longer periods and having a well-constructed portfolio helps a lot in this regard.

For those approaching or exceeding 30 years of age, having a medium-long term goal is advisable. Investing and setting aside money for retirement can be a good start.

To sum up the concept, everything depends on your time horizon:

- o If you think about using the money within one or three years, save it.

- o If you do not need this money for the next 10 years, invest it.

If, on the other hand, you plan on using the savings in the next 5 or 10 years, but you want to still have money set aside in your bank account, then you will have to do both. Keep in mind that this is much harder and requires more discipline. However, with the right mindset, it is certainly the best option.

What does trading wisely mean?

Since the importance of the investment is well established, it should also be emphasized that there is no recipe to guarantee the success of an investment.

However, following some prudential rules can help minimize risks.

First of all, we need to avoid the dream of making money overnight. On the market, there are professional operators, experts, who dedicate all their time to this activity, but they often make mistakes as well. Just to show how difficult it is and how "get rich quick schemes" do not exist.

One strategy that every investor needs to master to reduce the risk is diversification. This means not putting all your eggs in one basket, but spreading your resources on different assets. When the invested amount grows, it becomes more important to diversify not only between the asset classes (stocks, bonds, commodities) but also geographically (taking into account the currency variable) and size-wise (small or big cap companies to stay within the equity, more or less long maturities for government securities, bonds with different level of risk in the corporate sphere).

Making these choices takes time that needs to be subtracted from work or other activities. So, in the end, it is about investing time before moving the money. But it is worth it, and frankly speaking, the only option to avoid reckless choices that you may regret afterward.

Chapter 2

How Much Money You Need to Start Swing Trading?

Many people ask themselves this question: how much money do they need to invest in the forex market? An entirely legitimate question, but whose answer varies according to many factors. First of all, consider how you have decided to invest in currencies. The classic forex market requires capital of a certain size, usually including (at least) between $5,000 - $10,000 to start investing in the forex market.

If you do not have these figures or do not feel ready to invest them, you can use other financial instruments such as CFDs and binary options. In both cases, the minimum capital to invest is really limited. We usually speak of $100-200 to open an online trading account and have access to a trading platform to invest. Obviously, no one forbids you to start investing a larger amount. Our advice, especially if you have never done online trading before, is to invest a maximum of $1000 in your first CFD trading account or binary options.

Regardless of how you have decided to invest in the forex market, however, remember to choose only figures that you can afford to lose. What does it mean? It means that you have to invest in figures that will not put your financial stability at risk. In other words, do not invest "too big" figures for your pockets.

Another topic that must always be dealt with when it comes to investing in the forex market is the risk. Let's clarify it. Trading online, so investing in the forex market is risky. Risk is a factor that cannot be eliminated. Anyone who tells you that online trading and investing in the stock market is risk-free and easy is lying shamelessly. Trading online is risky, as it can result in the loss of your capital (in case of bad decisions).

Money Management and Risk

All investment activities are risky, whether the real estate market, opening a business or starting a start-up, or online trading, the risk is always present. The important thing is to know how to manage the risk factor so that it can be reduced and controlled. Nevertheless, remember that you will never be able to completely eliminate the risk factor. It will always be present in all your future forex exchange transactions.

This means that sooner or later, you will lose money by investing in the forex market. After all, no one is perfect: being able to make only profitable investments is impossible. We must accept the fact that suffering losses "is part of the game." But the important thing is to earn more than what you lose. If, for example, out of 10 investment transactions, you miss 2, but you earn from the remaining 8, you can say that you have reached an excellent goal (and profit).

Fix yourself with the idea of not wanting to lose money by investing in the stock market; it will not help if you want to start trading online. Professional investors know very well that losses must be accepted and need to aim towards limiting their number (check the term well: limit, do not eliminate). In this way, by limiting losses, profits will increase — the goal that every trader should operate on in the forex exchange.

What is the minimum capital requested to invest in the stock market? In this chapter, we will try to answer this question, with attention to the type of operation and market. First of all, we specify that when we talk about the minimum capital to invest in the stock market, we are talking about something very different from the minimum capital to invest in Forex. In fact, while the investment in Forex has an essentially speculative activity, in the stock exchange investment, dividends, coupons, and long-term investments are also to be assessed. Now, let's analyze how much it takes to invest in the stock market.

As mentioned, the minimum capital to invest in the stock market depends mainly on the type of operation that you intend to have. We can say with absolute certainty that the smaller the duration of the investment is, the less the required capital is. We will explain this statement in detail. If we operate with a maximum daily duration, it is presumable that every evening we close all open positions, so our minimum capital to invest in the stock market, even without leverage, may even be only $1,000 allowing at least one transaction per day. Operating with leverage, the minimum capital to invest in the stock exchange may be lower, even a few dollars if we use high leverage. It seems obvious that if the duration of our investment will be semi-annual, the minimum capital to invest in the stock market will have to be decidedly higher so as not to be in the sad condition of being able to operate once every six months.

So far, we have talked of minimum capital to invest in the stock market exclusively from the point of view of the number of possible transactions. However, it is not so simple. The minimum capital to invest in the stock market should be sufficient to diversify our exposure to avoid large losses. The ideal situation would be to invest in at least three markets with only two market transactions. It goes without saying that with a very short duration leverage operation, the minimum capital to invest in the stock market will be from a few thousand dollars, while for half-year transactions the capital will necessarily have to be higher. Obviously, so far we have talked about optimal operations. The minimum capital to invest in the stock market will depend very much on your risk profile. The greater your risk appetite, the higher your leverage will be, and therefore you will be able to invest with a smaller capital.

Chapter 3

An Introduction to Swing Trading and the Basic Strategies to Make Money in the Market

Most beginner investors and traders have relatively confused ideas when approaching the forex market, trading currencies (or options, ETFs, commodities, etc.), or trading in general.

One of the pivotal points that create confusion in the mind of those interested in making their money work through investments is the lack of understanding and the crucial difference that exists between trading and investing.

The confusion derives from the fact that in the eyes of the investor or the uneducated and non-conscious trader, doing trading or investing seems to be the same thing.

In reality, although the desire to make a profit unites them, the two operations arise from different logics and follow different rules.

In fact, those who invest in a measure of the value of what they buy (an action, a house, a business, an object of art, etc.), try to buy it at a discounted or otherwise balanced price, and the entire operation is based on the prediction or hope that, over time, the good purchased will increase in value and that this increase in value will automatically be reflected in a corresponding increase in its market price allowing it to be sold for a profit.

An easily understandable example of investment is that of those who buy agricultural land in the expectation that it will then be buildable.

The greatest investors of history, such as the legendary Warren Buffett, are in fact masters in buying "depreciated quality." Of course, their time horizon is never very short, and the value of what they have purchased can remain or even go down for a certain period of time without this causing them to worry excessively.

Who trades, however, does not bet on a change in the value of things. To be honest, the hard and pure forex trader does not care highly about the objective quality or the nature of what he buys. He is only interested in acquiring it at a price that (in a generally rather short time frame) he plans to grow, regardless of the fact that the value of what he purchased remains perfectly identical.

In fact, what makes trading possible is simply the fact that the prices of things (and therefore also investment objects such as shares, bonds, real estate, etc.) may vary irrespective of their value due to the law of the application and the offer.

An example out of context of activity comparable to trading is that of the Super Bowl tickets reseller, who obtains the tickets three weeks earlier at regular prices and then resells them at the last moment when lacking tickets and many questions, he can market them to a much higher price.

On an exchange, for an investor, it is crucial to understand what he is buying and what the current and future value of the company he is planning to buy shares is. In other words, investors search quality companies that are currently depreciated.

On the other hand, for a forex trader, it is sufficient to use tools (generally the stock's graph evaluated through technical analysis) that allow him to make a forecast of the future price of the stock regardless of the value of the company and its corporate purpose.

To start trading, you must meet the following requirements:

- a PC with a stable internet connection
- an online trading platform, to be chosen among those recommended and regulated by us
- all the recommended brokers offer an adequate training to all traders whether they are novice traders or experts
- graphs relating to market quotes in real time
- economic news
- comments and operational suggestions
- a great desire to learn

Today, thanks to online trading, it will be possible to obtain profits that can reach up to 70% based on the chosen broker and a fair-trading preparation, without which one risks losing the entire capital invested. Therefore, we advise you to scrupulously apply and follow all the advice that your broker provides you.

In addition, thanks to the many materials that can be found in this book, you can start learning what are the right terms of online trading, how you can invest in the forex market, etc.

When investing in the forex market, you can do mainly two different types of transactions:

- Long operations (upward investment)
- Short transactions (downward investment)

In other words, when you are trading, you can buy currencies and sell currencies. The goal, however, remains the same: to make a profit. When you want to buy, you will only get a profit if the value of the currency will be increased when we want to sell it. For example, we buy 100 lots of a currency when it is worth $1.1 each, and then we sell them when they're worth $1.2 each. The price difference multiplied by the number of lots equals our profit.

When you want to sell, it becomes a bit more complicated. In short transactions, in fact, it is the broker that lends us the number of shares on which we want to invest on the downside. For example, the broker can lend us 1000 euros listed at $1.23 each. The securities that the broker lends us for a short transaction are sold immediately: the profit remains "frozen" in their trading account.

This profit will be used to buy back the same amount of currency that the broker had lent us because we have to return these currencies to the broker. In that case, we will have a gain if the value of the currency has fallen.

The difference between the initial sale of the securities lent and the expense to repurchase them is + $500 in this case. That is our profit. If, on the other hand, the value of the currency increases, we will have to spend more money than those earned from the initial sale of the prearranged securities — in this case, we will suffer a loss.

Chapter 4

The Right Mental Mindset to Have

Let's not hide behind the common opinion that you do not have money to invest. Do not get us wrong; you may be in the situation where money is tight, and you do not have the resources to make a decisive move in the market. However, you can always control your cash flow and add extra streams of income. These will provide you with more money that you need to save for future investments. We know it is hard, but it is possible, and most millionaires started with nothing.

To us, mindset is extremely valuable, and in this chapter, we want to debunk once and for all the most recurring excuses people use to avoid or postpone their investments.

1. "I do not have time to trade."
One of the most common excuses is to believe that investing can take away most of the precious time we have available. The truth is that we are committing a big error of assessment. Trading does not require a specific amount of time: you can choose how much time you want to dedicate to it. Obviously, the more, the better, but you can even start with few minutes a day.

Thanks to the advent of the internet and new technologies, in fact, investing is now just a click away, thus reducing not only the costs of negotiation but also the time required.

2. "I do not have enough money to trade."
To believe that investing is a subject reserved for those with large quantities of money is one of the worst mistakes we can make. Let's dispel this myth immediately: it is not true that to make money, we need big money. There are affordable financial

products that do not require the fortunes of Scrooge McDuck to start planning your future.

From today, it is possible to start trading and investing starting from just 5 euros.

Think about it, 5 dollars equals 5 coffees a week. If we had saved a coffee a day for 5 days a week since the euros came into force, until the end of 2019, we would have put aside a "small" sum of $3865. If these savings, instead of being forgotten in our piggy bank, were invested in global equity markets, at the end of 2019 we would have had $7493. No savings are therefore insignificant to be invested.

3. "I do not have the skills to trade."

One of the reasons that drive us away from investing is to convince ourselves that we do not have the right skills and knowledge. Trading in the forex market may seem apparently difficult, but the truth is that you do not have to be Warren Buffett to start doing it. By investing in mutual funds, for example, our savings are entrusted to a team of expert managers who make the investment choices for us on a daily basis. While we let others manage our money, it is fundamental to learn. Remember that the goal is to become an investor that takes care of his resources.

4. "I will trade in a few years when I have a higher salary."

Delaying an investment is not a wise choice, especially considering the benefits of compound interest capitalization. To show you, we have compared two capital accumulation plans: the first invests a sum of $100 a month from the age of 25, while the second invests $200 a month but starts from 35 years.

In your opinion, which of the two will be able to obtain a higher capital at the age of 70?

The accumulation plan of $100 monthly, undertaken since 25 years, will have generated at the age of 70 a capital of 520,000 dollars: 50,000 more than the other.

Anticipating the investment not only requires less economic effort but also allows you to obtain higher earnings compared to a higher investment delayed over time.

5. "Trading is too risky."

None of us wants to lose money, but we do not realize that we are already doing this when we decide not to trade. If the alternative to investing is, in fact, to feel safe by parking our savings on the bank account, inflation could reserve us unpleasant surprises reducing inexorably our purchasing power in the future.

If you trade using portfolio diversification and adopting a long-term time horizon, the chances of losing money are reduced a lot.

When it comes to trading strategies, the amount invested cannot be ignored.
This chapter is oriented to the management of assets between 10,000 and one million euros. Another premise for reading is to have a clear idea of what is meant by the amount investable.

We will divide our field of action into three bands. All three bands will assume that it has already been done:

- trade the maximum tax-deductible share in the supplementary pension;
- stipulate any life insurance; and indicates that all the negative points described in Life Insurance should be considered;
- deduct from the tradable portion any allowances for false investments, i.e., secondary activities that are genuine alternative works.

The last point is particularly important for investments in real estate and land. As we will see in the operational plans, for assets up to $250,000 a speech on property and land can only be marginal.

The main reasons for the previous statement are:

1. Such trades often tend not to be real.

In the modern sense, an investment is such if it requires a minimum allocation of resources (for example, I buy 10,000 dollars of government bonds); otherwise, it is configured as a real activity.

Buying a home that you then rent is the simplest example.

If we interact directly with the tenant, we are doing a real activity, an alternative to our work, in which we often do not take into account the management costs and the time we spend; different is the case in which we limit ourselves to buying the house and entrust to a paid external structure the role of administrator of the building. In this second case, what remains is the real gain of the rent. The same applies when buying agricultural land: only by considering it an activity (i.e., cultivating it and managing it with appropriate decisions) will we be able to make the most of it.

2. These trades minimize management costs only for large capital.

In fact, the realized capital gains are gross of the taxes and of all the management expenses that serve to maintain the asset in question over the years. For small investments (for example a house worth 300,000 dollars) inflation, taxes, maintenance costs, etc. they reduce the real gain considerably.

Trading instruments

As investment tools consider:

1. properties and land
2. instruments for maximum liquidity (i.e., liquidable in up to 3 months)
3. bonds
4. stocks
5. Currencies (Forex)

The individual instruments must then be optimized following the instructions given in the following paragraphs.

We must warn against investing in alternative and typically speculative fields (art, jewelry, etc.) without having a specific capacity. These fields are in fact similar to alternative work: buying a painting, a prestigious watch or a classic car, hoping for a great revaluation, is completely optimistic if you are not an expert in the sector. On the other hand, if one is, it makes no sense to make it all occasional, but it would make sense to make it at least a second activity.

The proposed managements are mainly passive, in the sense that we must follow the trend of our trades not continuously over time, but with periodic checks (for example quarterly) to verify whether it is appropriate to positively disinvest. For example, if a currency was bought a year ago at 95.25 and is now worth 99, a 4% gain justifies the sale. If, on the contrary, it has fallen to 94.20, it will put the heart in peace and will be held until its expiration.

From 10,000 to 50,000 euros

I know I am disappointed by those who thought of diversifying, but with such a modest sum, you can only use two tools: forex and bonds. You can use together or better use the latter unless the former is no longer advantageous due to a particular economic situation.

From 50,000 to 250,000 euros

Here the four instruments are all usable, obviously with due consideration.

For buildings and land, it is advisable to include them in the additional quota. If you decide to invest 50,000 dollars in real estate, instead of buying a tiny studio, it makes more sense to buy a bigger house of ownership.

The fees on the added quota are less than on a second home, and there would not be all the hassles of managing an asset, which due to its small size would yield modest yields in any case of a certain management commitment.

Also, in this case, the bonds take the largest share of the investable amount (at least 50%) and can be replaced by the instruments for maximum liquidity only in exceptional cases in which they make more.

The actions deserve separate speech. In theory, with a capital of $250,000, it would be possible to invest in the shareholder, but in practice, it is better to do so by linking the figure to one's age.

If at 30 years, an invested share of 40% can be significant, at the age of 60, it should not exceed 10%. With these data, it is automatic to remember that at the age of 40, a maximum of 30% is invested and at most 20% a maximum of 20%.

Let us remember, however, that investing in the stock is an opportunity, not an obligation.

From 250,000 to one million euros

We are now in important figures. Before going into detail, it is necessary to understand "what wind it pulls." Currently, with an economy still in partial crisis, it seems that the situation is this:

secure bonds and liquidity: ****
actions: **
gold: **
properties: *

This picture will appear disappointing to those who dream of speculating with their capital, but it is certainly the one that protects it most. For those people, forex might not be the best option.

With regard to property and land, up to 30% of assets can be invested in them, both as an additional share and as an investment in its own right. Many would come to invest up to 100%, but it is a too simplistic solution because, in fact, with such capital, if you want to invest in the brick, it makes more sense to undertake a real second activity. Furthermore, it should be remembered that *a property has value only if you can resell it!*

What in recent years has not been so easy and has produced losses of even 50%, just to fall from the investment made with a little liquidity.

In other words, instead of investing in a couple of luxury apartments in the city center, it is more logical to invest in smaller units by diversifying the risks that are always present on the individual investment. In any case, the crisis in the real estate sector that began in 2008 has, in fact, extinguished optimism that lasted for decades, optimism without a real rational motivation.

Once the portion allocated to property and land has been determined, the amount to be invested in shares must be determined. Also, in this case, the maximum is represented by the rule of 70. The remaining part is destined to the bonds.

Chapter 5

Stacking Up Money and Increasing the Funds

Earning more means being paid more. We usually think that others should pay us more if we want to make more money. But this is not always true: we can earn more even if we pay ourselves more, and not the others.

This is a fundamental principle underlying the financial success, first disclosed in 1926 by George Samuel Clason through his book entitled *The Richest Man in Babylon*, a great motivational classic.

The principle states that part of what you earn must be maintained. Putting aside at least 10% of what you earn - and making that money inaccessible to ordinary expenses and possibly even extraordinary expenses - you can increase this amount exponentially over time. Considering any investments, thanks to the power of the compound investment, the amount saved/invested - over the years - can become important. In fact, many people are able to earn more and build their assets by paying themselves first. It is a true and effective principle today as it was in 1926.

Yet, as this 10% formula is easy, people are unwilling to listen to it and apply it. This is because you are usually looking for tricks to get rich quickly, and you do not have a medium to long-term vision. On the other hand, having a long-term investment plan is a solid foundation on which to build one's own economic stability. And you can start earning more by paying yourself first from today. The earlier you start and the quicker you will build your financial success.

Using the power of compound interest
To earn more, you can take advantage of the compound interest. Here's how it works: if you invest 1,000 dollars at a 5% interest, you will earn 50 dollars of interest, and at the end of the first year, you will

have a total investment of 1,050 dollars. If you leave both the initial investment and the interest earned on the current account, you will receive a 5% interest the following year over $ 1,050, or $ 52.50. In the third year, you will earn 5% out of 1.102.50, and so on. At this rate, within 15-30 years your money will turn into an amount well above the sum invested initially. But precisely how much does the invested capital grow? The Italian mathematician Luca Pacioli explained it in the fifteenth century: any capital doubles in a number of years equal to 72 divided by the interest rate. Returning to our example: if the interest is at 5% per year, we divide 72 by 5; which makes 14.4, i.e., in 14 years and 4 months the initial capital doubles. The sooner you start and the bigger the result will be, as you will have more time for the interest you capitalize to produce its powerful magic. Start now to save and invest for your future, even if you do not have a large sum. You do not need to have an extra sum of money. You can start with any amount and grow it over time.

The secret of paying of yourself first

If you want to earn more money by paying yourself first, you have to make savings and investment a central part of your financial management, just like the mortgage payment. Get accustomed to saving a fixed percentage (at least 10%) of your monthly income and investing it in a special savings account that you decide not to touch. Ideally, this step would be automatic, such as a fixed monthly deduction on your paycheck. The automation will ensure that you will not have to rely on your self-discipline and your ability to save will not be affected by your mood, from domestic emergencies or otherwise. Continue to increase that account until you have saved enough to invest the sum accumulated in bonds, in a mutual fund or real estate (spending money on rent without building any assets is really a waste). Let your investments build your assets over time, and try to live with what remains after you have paid yourself. If you want to spend, try to earn more to afford it. But never put your hands on your savings to finance a more ambitious lifestyle. The ideal would be for your investments to grow to the point where you could live with interest, if necessary. Only then will you really be financially autonomous and free.

If you want to earn more, you need to create assets, not liabilities. Rather than spending all the money you earn, by enriching someone else, invest in assets that produce other income (stocks, bonds, real estate, gold, etc.). Then when your money starts to grow, educate yourself further about the best way to invest your money. Stay informed about news about investment opportunities and remember to protect what is yours through a good insurance policy. Do not blindly trust who will manage your money, but always try to improve your financial education. This will make you a financially prepared person ready to get rich. Once you understand this, money will follow.

What is compound interest? Not everyone may know how to respond immediately to this question. In fact, if everyone knows what the simple interest is, i.e., the one that withdraws at the end of the agreed time unit, fewer are those who know what the compound interest is, how it works and, most importantly, how to take advantage of it.

The example of a bank account is enlightening.

If on 1 January I have a net rate of 1% on my account, at the end of the year I have 101 euros. The euro more is added to the capital and, if the conditions do not change, at the end of the second year I will not have 102 euros, but 102 euros and 1 cent where the cent represents 1% of the euro accumulated after the first year.

So far, everything is clear, but most of us cannot calculate the compound interest of an investment and tend to treat it as simple interest. This is due to its slow start, that, especially with small capital, tend to be treated as "irrelevant." However, there is nothing more wrong that an investor could do.

If, for example, after 5 years of investment, my capital of 100 euros is now 140, we are led to believe that the interest was 8% per year.

This is incorrect because, in doing so, we do not take into account that at the end of each period the interest accumulate has gone to increase capital. If the interest had really been 8%, composing the 5 years, we would have had

Initial capital: 100

- 1st year: 108
- 2nd year: 116.64
- 3rd year: 125.97
- 4th year: 136.04
- 5th year: 146.93

The difference (6.93 euros) represents almost 7% of the total. As you can see, it is easy to take dazzle (and worse, even "suffer," if for some reason we are offered a simple interest for a compound interest).

The math behind compound interest: an easy example

Suppose we have an initial capital of 1,000 euros. The capital yields a Y% interest and this interest is calculated on an annual basis.

What will be the value of the investment after X years?

The calculation formula is as follows:

(1) IV = CP (1 + Y) ^ X

IV is the value of the investment after X years, while CP is the initial capital. Y is expressed as a percentage, i.e., 0.04 indicates 4%. The symbol ^ is the symbol of elevation to power.

The inverse calculation tends to find the Y interest of an investment that now (net of inflation) is worth IV against a CP capital invested X periods (years) ago. The formula is:

$$(2)\ Y = (IV / CP) \wedge (1 / X) - 1$$

Suppose that, after inflation, 1,000 euros invested 5 years ago are now worth 1,400 euros, you immediately have that the yield was 6.96%.

Let's take a look at another example
Marie has just taken the salary and can finally buy the air conditioner she needs.

But her friend Julie calls her to tell her that she has an urgent need that she cannot cope with immediately and asks her to borrow $ 1,000.

Marie is undecided because this would mean waiting another month before she can make her purchase.

To resolve the issue, the two girls agree on the loan provided that Julie returns the money to Mary with a 5% interest (the numbers are purely random for the purposes of the example).

In this way, Marie has a greater incentive to have to delay her purchase.

When Julie returns the sum loaned, she will receive $ 1,050 instead of $ 1,000.

The following month Marie can then buy the air conditioner and, to celebrate, use the $ 50 interest to go out to dinner with her boyfriend.

In short, in the end, this recognition for the delayed use was not bad!

Now that we understand the concept behind the rate of interest it is good to enter a little more in detail and make some distinctions.

In this regard, we can divide the interest rate into two broad categories:

1. The simple interest;
2. The compound interest.

Simple Interest

Let's go back to the previous example.

At the end of the period, Julie returns the money plus the interest to Mary. Soon after, however, the girl asks again the same amount to buy a new refrigerator, as the old one suddenly broke.

Marie agrees to lend the money back to her friend.

The following month Julie firmed up her debt plus new interests, again for a total of $ 1,050.

Now Marie is with her initial capital, plus $ 100 in interest, for a total of $ 1,100.

Interest is defined as simple when, once it has matured on the underlying capital, it does not generate further interest.

In our example, we note that the first 50 $ were not added to the capital loaned the second time.

Compound Interest

Change of scenery.

Julie asks Marie to lend her $ 1,000 with the promise to return them in two years.

Mary agrees, as long as Julie accepts a compound interest on the mature borrowed capital.

In this case, Julie will not have to pay the interest immediately at the end of the 1st year but will add the $ 50 interest in the capital, which in turn will accumulate 5% in the 2nd year.

At the end of the agreed period, Julie must therefore return:

- o $ 1,000 capital
- o $ 50 interest for the first year ($ 1,000 + 5%)
- o $ 52.50 interest for the 2nd year ($ 1.050 + 5%)

The total capital to be returned to Mary is, therefore, $ 1,102.50.

Here we have materialized $ 2.50 more than the previous example, due to the compound interest.

The interest is defined as compound when, once it has matured on the underlying capital, it is added to the latter and contributes to generate further increased interest in the future.

Do you understand why the compound interest is your new best friend?

When you deposit your money in the bank account you are doing as Marie, that is, you are "lending" your money to the bank, which uses them to perform its credit function and lend it to people and businesses.
As a reward for this service, you are given an interest in the sums deposited, that is, a reward for the fact that you delay their use.

How to take advantage of the compound interest
If you do not want inflation to eat a nice slice of the real value and the purchasing power of your money, you have to make sure that the latter accrue compound interest over time.

Certainly, a part of the liquidity at your disposal you can deposit on one or more deposit accounts, or accounts with limited operations, where however higher interest rates are recognized.

For example, you could deposit your emergency fund. The rest, however, you should invest in a portfolio of efficient financial instruments that protect your capital and create added value.

The compound interest must, therefore, be exploited for at least two reasons:

1. Increase savings while waiting for their use;
2. Defense against inflation.

A wise thing to do is, therefore, exploit the power of compound interest to make the value of your money grow faster, protecting it from loss of purchasing power.
Try to keep only small amounts on bank accounts that give you little to nothing.
You can leave just the right liquidity for your daily expenses and the emergency fund.

Chapter 6

Different Types of Trading Strategies and The Importance of Leverage

What is leverage? Through the use of financial leverage a person has the possibility to buy or sell financial assets for an amount higher than the capital held and, consequently, to benefit from a higher potential return than that deriving from a direct investment in the underlying and, conversely, to expose himself to the risk of very significant losses.

How does the leverage work?

Let's see how the concept of leverage works starting from a simple case. Let's assume you have $ 100 available to invest in a currency pair. Let's assume that the gain or loss expectations are equal to 30%: if things go well, we will have $ 130; otherwise, we will have $ 70. This is a simple speculation in which we bet on a particular event.

In case we decide to risk more for our investment, in addition to our $ 100, also another $ 900 borrowed, then the investment would take a different articulation because we use a leverage of 10 to 1 (we invest $ 1000 having a capital initial only of 100). If things go well and the stock goes up 30%, we will receive $ 1300; we return the 900 borrowed with a gain of $ 300 on an initial capital of 100. So we get a 300% profit with a stock that only gave a 30% return. Obviously, on the $ 900 borrowed we will have to pay an interest, but the general principle remains valid: the leverage makes it possible to increase the possible gains.

Considering the further case of the investment in derivatives. Let's assume we buy a future that, within a month, gives the right to buy 100 grams of gold at a price set today of $ 5,000. We could physically buy the gold with an outlay of 5000 $ and keep it waiting for the price to rise and then sell it back. If we decide instead to use derivatives, we should not have $ 5,000, but only the capital needed to buy the derivative. Let's say that a bank sells for 100 $ the derivative that allows us to buy the same 100 grams of gold in a month to $ 5,000. If in a month the gold is worth 5,500, we can buy it and sell it immediately, realizing a gain of 500 $. With the 100 $ of the price of the derivative, we make a profit of $ 400, or 400%, with $ 100.

This is how leverage works. Do you get the amazing power it can give to the average investor?

What are the potentials of its use?
The potential of leveraging is clear. But be careful: the leverage multiplier effect, described with the previous examples, works even if the investment goes wrong. For example, if we decide to invest $ 100 in our possession plus an additional sum of $ 900 borrowed, if the currency pair depreciated by 30%, we would remain with only $ 700 in hand; having to return the $

900 borrowed plus interest and considering the $ 100 of our initial investment we would have a loss of over $ 300 on an initial capital of $ 100. As a percentage, the loss would, therefore, be 300% against a reduction in the value of the pair of 30%.

Another element to keep in mind is that the different financial levers can be combined: in this way speculation operations are carried out using a "squared lever" with clear reflections on potential potentials.

What are the risks related to leverage?

What may appear to be an interesting tool with positive potential for the investor, on the other hand, presents risks that must, therefore, be taken into due consideration. In fact, if the financial system as a whole works with a very high leverage and financial institutions lend money to each other to multiply the possible profits, the loss of an individual investor can trigger a domino effect by infecting the entire financial market.

Banks are typically entities that operate with a more or less high degree of leverage: against a certain net capital, the total assets in which the resources are invested is generally much higher. For example, a bank with equity of $ 100 and leverage of 20 manages assets for $ 2,000. A loss of 1% of the assets involves the loss of 20% of the equity capital.

The development of the market for the transfer of credit risk (from financial intermediaries to the market) has meant that the traditional bank model, called "originate-and-hold" ("create and hold": the bank that provided the loan it remains in the balance sheet until maturity), has been substituted for many operators from the "originate-to-distribute" ("create and distribute": the intermediary selects the debtors, but then transfers the loan to others, recovering the liquidity and the regulatory capital previously committed or the pure credit risk, with benefits only on capital requirements), with the effect of a further increase in leverage. The spread of this second bank model is one of the factors that explain the crisis triggered on the sub-prime mortgage market.

Property price inflation has supported the issuance of loans and the exponential growth of the related market, allowing banks to make huge profits and, at the same time, increase leverage. But "the money machine" could not last long and in the end, many banks found themselves without sufficient capital to absorb the losses deriving from the inversion of the real estate market trend, resulting in fact in failed companies.

In the meantime, the example of the banks has spread within the financial system by spreading to all other financial institutions: leverage had prevailed, especially in the United States, generating a huge volume of risky investments that rested on a fraction infinitesimal of equity capital. We are thinking of the issue of so-called "credit default swaps" (derivative instruments used to hedge against the default risk of the debtor): some insurance companies were heavily exposed to the real estate market, and when the latter collapsed, and the value of mortgages fell, they began to lose without having sufficient capital to absorb the losses deriving from the issue of those instruments.

In order not to risk failing and return to sufficient levels of bank capital, capital increases (not an easy task in times of crisis), the reduction of the amount of loans to businesses (granting a lower number of new loans and not renewal of those already issued) and the disposal of other liquid assets (mostly shares) can be used. The result of all this, in the period of the sub-prime crisis, was a credit freeze and a collapse of the stock market. These are the main channels through which the financial crisis has hit the real economy. Credit rationing has affected investments, and the decline in the stock market (which adds to the decline in house prices) has reduced the value of household wealth and therefore consumption.

We know that a certain level of leverage is physiological to sustain economic growth, even if we have no indication of what the optimal level is. But history teaches us how in an increasingly globalized and interdependent economic-financial system, leverage can be a trigger for speculative bubbles. And it is in these periods that the strongest disconnect between finance and the real economy is generated.

Now that we have gone through the power of leverage, it is time to take a look at what we call the 30 Secrets Rules of trading and how see how they can be applied to the different financial instruments.

1. *"If you are undecided, stay still."* It is not necessary to invest continuously. If you do not have precise ideas, it is better to do nothing and wait for clearer signs. Often times, the market is full of indecision: keep calm and stack up money for the future.

2. *"Cut losses and let profits run."* This is perhaps the best known and most important rule for those investing in the stock market. An indispensable factor for the application of this rule is the identification, immediately after the purchase, of the stop loss. This is how much you are willing to lose on that investment (take into account when determining the average daily excursion of the stock). The cold and systematic application, even if painful, of the stop loss will preserve you from huge losses that would make

the sale more and more traumatic, freezing capital that could be invested elsewhere.

3. *"Learn from your mistakes."* Errors are not always negative: if you follow a strategy with a method, if you apply the stop losses, you will not make particularly serious mistakes. Errors are an integral part of stock trading: you need to analyze why you made them and what you can learn from them. In this way, a small loss can become a good investment lesson for the future.

4. *"Take profit and invest them back."* If one of our titles is on the rise, take profit will be applied as the stock grows. A stock cannot grow indefinitely, when the trend is reversed, selling at the top, we will have had a profit avoiding further descents. If then the title should go up again, it does not matter; it will go better next time. You cannot always sell at the top since remember, you cannot time the market.

5. *"Buy on the rumor and sell on the news."* When positive news on a certain title officially come out, pay attention. It may already be too late to invest in that title since the market could already have priced it in.

6. *Do not believe in "safe investments."* If someone tells you that a title will certainly reach a certain price, he either does not understand much of the stock market or is only doing his own interests.

7. *"Never become emotionally attached to a stock."* Some investors always follow a limited number of companies that they consider more reliable than others. There are no titles better than others, but only favorable situations and unfavorable situations. Often, instead of admitting an error, one perseveres on it with the consequence of being heavily unbalanced on a stock. This is really bad, especially if you are overcommitted to a stock in which, at that moment, the market does not believe in.

8. *"Always maintain a certain liquidity available."* Cyclically we find ourselves in situations of several days of generalized decline of the whole stock exchange and often, for lack of liquidity, we cannot grasp excellent buying opportunities. Keep some money aside to jump on big opportunities.

9. *"Choose the right platform."* One important rule for investing in the stock market is that the platform makes the difference. Carefully selecting safe, honest and reliable trading platforms is the first step to make money. Those who start investing in the stock market for the first time must be careful to choose platforms that are really simple to use, perhaps with a high-quality educational support. Some platforms also offer add-on tools, such as notifications, social trading, and free analysis tools, to guide less experienced traders.

10. *"Invest only in what you understand."* As the "guru" of finance, Warren Buffett said, "never, never, invest in something that you do not

understand, and above all, that you do not know." The overwhelming majority of investors can achieve their capital growth goals by using the most common financial instruments, which are almost always simple to understand. The complex tools are best left to the great experts in the field.

11. *"Diversify your portfolio."* When investing, the word to keep in mind is "diversification." Never invest in a single title, because if that sinks, your money will come to the same end. It is always better to have diversified investments to minimize the specific risks of a company, a market, an asset class or a currency. The more you diversify and the lower the probability of having drastic falls.

12. *"Understand and evaluate the risk."* Risk is an intrinsic component of every investment. If it does not exist, there is no return. Whether they are government bonds, stocks or mutual funds, they all have a risk component, which will obviously be greater if you want to hope for

higher returns. So, if someone tells you that there is an investment without risk, it means that it is better to get advice from someone else.

13. *"Look beyond direct investment."* As an alternative to direct purchase of shares, it is possible to invest in the stock market indexes, through ETFs (listed mutual funds, which replicate the performance of equity and bond indices), or in mutual funds, that offer a high diversification even with minimum amounts, allow you to invest small periodic shares, for example, 100 euros per month, and may even provide a monthly coupon.

14. *"Do not follow the masses."* The typical decision of who buys stocks by investing in the stock market is usually strongly influenced by the advice of acquaintances, neighbors or relatives. So, if everyone around is investing in a particular company, a beginner investor tends to do the same. But this strategy is bound to fail in the long run, and it is not the right approach. There should be no need to say that you should

always avoid having a herd mentality if you do not want to lose hard-earned money on the stock market. The world's biggest investor, Warren Buffett, is right when he says "Be fearful when others are greedy, and be greedy when others are fearful!"

15. *"Do not try to time the market."* One thing that Warren Buffett does not do is try to time the stock market, even if he has a very strong understanding of the key price levels of the single shares. Most investors, however, do exactly the opposite, which often causes losses of money. So, you should never try to give timing the market a chance. In reality, no one has ever succeeded in doing so successfully and consistently over multiple market cycles.

16. *"Be disciplined."* Historically, it has often happened that during periods of high market upswing, we first caused moments of panic. Market volatility has inevitably made investors poorer, even if the market moved in the intended direction. Therefore, it is prudent to

have patience and follow a disciplined investment approach as well as keeping a long-term general picture in mind.

17. *"Be realistic and do not hope."* There is nothing wrong with hoping to make the best investment, but you could be in trouble if the financial goals are not based on realistic assumptions. For example, many stocks have generated more than 50 percent of returns during the big uptrend in recent years. However, this does not mean that we can always expect the same kind of return from the stock exchange.

18. *"Keep your portfolio under control."* We live in a connected world. Every important event that happens anywhere in the world also has an impact on our money. So we have to constantly monitor our portfolio and make adjustments.

19. *"Be sure to be on the legal side of things."* If someone proposes an investment, it must be verified as an "authorized project." In our

country, those who offer financial investments must be authorized by law, and this is an important safeguard for savers. In fact, the authorization is issued only in the presence of the requested requisites and, once authorized, the financial intermediaries are subject to constant supervision. Checking this is not particularly demanding: if you have internet you can even directly access the information held by the supervisory authorities; otherwise you can contact the authorities themselves using traditional means.

20. *"Be skeptical and do your own research."* Nobody gives anything for nothing: be wary of investment proposals that ensure a very high return. At the promise of high returns, there are usually very high risks or, in some cases, even attempts of fraud. Be wary of "Ponzi schemes" which promise profits linked to the subsequent adhesion of other subjects, who often must be convinced by the investor himself to join. These "operations," in fact, cannot guarantee any kind of return, as they are normally supplied

exclusively by the continuity of the accessions. In other words, when the new signatures are no longer sufficient to pay the "interests" to the previous subscribers, the schemes are destined to fail. Be wary of the vague and generic investment proposals, for which the methods for using the money collected are not explained in detail (what kind of securities will be purchased, at what prices, on which markets, with which risk profiles - interest rate, foreign exchange or counterparty - and whether and which hedging instruments will be used to cover such risks).

21. *"Have a long-term mindset."* According to Warren Buffett, the shares once bought, are not to be sold. It is, therefore, better to evaluate the industrial trends in the long term and then buy them, leaving aside the passengers' enthusiasm.

22. *"When investing in real estate, know the area you are investing in."* To start with, it is good that you put your focus on your area of residence or, if you live in a big city, even on your neighborhood or on one that you know

well. If you think to act on a field of action too large, you risk dispersing too much energy towards something that can present totally different solutions. Dedicate yourself only to residential buildings, apartments or houses. The commercial ones, even if they can be very profitable, have other rules and in general greater difficulties. The same for the land: you can do big business, but it is not something suitable for those who start.

23. *"Choose the right leverage and use it to your advantage."* Real estate investments must be done with leverage. If you want to make an investment only with your money, then the essence of real estate investment is not clear to you. In fact, the concept of financial leverage allows you to invest with money that is not yours but to make money directly for you. Leverage an economic tool that allows you to get where you would not get only with your own strength. You can take out a mortgage (if you can afford it) or engage financial partners. It may seem strange to you but it is not at all: even

the richest need partners and remember that a figure that seems almost unimaginable to you, it may be normal to somebody else.

24. *"Verba volant, scripta manent"* the Latins used to say. So never make verbal agreements, even if it is a relative or a childhood friend. Consult a lawyer to have the templates of the documents to be used. Like everything, at first it will seem difficult, but after a few times you will become an expert in basic legal practices for the sale of real estate, and you will be able to create documents in a very short time even by yourself.

25. *"Consider shorter positions."* In the fixed income universe, a short duration approach is potentially able to reduce sensitivity to rising interest rates, while optimizing the returns/risk rations.

26. *"Know your risk/reward ratio."* A higher return may be tempting, but you must be sure not to take too many risks in relation to the

remuneration you would get. In bond markets, this means avoiding lengthening duration in a context of rising interest rates. Increasing investments in riskier assets may seem appropriate at the moment when the macroeconomic scenario is quite positive, but it could turn out to be a rather risky choice if the situation should change. For example, the yields offered by high yield debt, on average 3% in Europe and 5.5% in the United States, would not be sufficient to compensate investors if insolvencies passed from their current level of 2% to a more normal one of the 5%. Conversely, market areas with a good risk/return profile, with high-rated issuers offering attractive returns, include emerging market debt, subordinated financial bonds, and hybrid corporate bonds. Aiming at long-term quality makes it possible to take on fair risks, helping to limit the impact of any negative macroeconomic event.

27. *"Take the currency pairing into account."*
Global investments expose to currency risks.

High yield bonds and emerging market funds, for example, are usually denominated in US dollars, but the underlying bonds they hold may be issued in another currency. Fund managers may choose to include currency risk in the overall portfolio risk as exchange rates fluctuate, or decide to contain this risk through currency hedging.

28. *"Stay flexible, keep some cash aside."* It is important to have the flexibility to underwrite and liquidate investments to seize the best opportunities. However, trades are expensive and can quickly erode earnings. This happens above all in the bond markets, given the relatively low levels of returns. The bid-ask spread is on average 30-40% of the yield, so an excess of trades erodes this margin and obviously reduces the total return. Even holding portfolios with structurally short duration, allowing short-term bonds to come to maturity naturally, can improve returns because you will effectively pay the bid-ask spread once.

29. *"Build up your portfolio over time."* If investing a small sum such as 5000 Euro, will not allow you to live on that income, it can certainly represent an opportunity, to make money. In addition, even if you have a good economic availability, the ideal is always "to take it safe," starting investing from small figures and then fuel the investment over time.

30. *"The past does not equal the future."* The story is not indicative of how an investment will result in the future and investors should always try to weigh the potential risks associated with a particular investment, as well as its possible returns.

All these strategies and rules can easily be applied to swing trading, which is when you trade on market swings (meaning you take advantage of long movements), option trading (meaning you earn as long as the market stays in a specific range) and forex, which is when you trade the different currencies.

Chapter 7

Swing Trading Crypto

One of the strategies that I am going to explain to you is trading in cryptocurrency. Why do we invest mainly in crypto and blockchain related assets? Because we truly believe they are one of the biggest undergoing revolution at this very moment and that this is the perfect time to get involved before the market explodes to the upside and prices rise at major stocks level.

Another reason that I like cryptocurrencies and their market is that they are extremely volatile and provide the average Joe the possibility to make serious money without investing a lot. It is not a secret, in fact, that every time the market starts to rise, people rush into the search for the "next big win" and the question that circulates is always the same: "What will the next cryptocurrency be that will go to 'the moon'?"

The issue with cryptocurrencies is that being a market that is not yet regulated in several countries, the risk of pumps and dumps, manipulation and fraud is just around the corner. This is why I wanted to cover them in this book. In fact, since they provide a great opportunity, I am worried that a lot of people may get involved without knowing what they are doing and will lose a lot of money down the line. Here I want to show you what I do before investing in a particular asset and how I keep it a sustainable source of passive income.

Before getting started, here is a list of useful tools for the analysis of cryptocurrencies:

- Coincheckup.com - one of my favorite sites, offers much more data than other cryptocurrency monitoring sites;
- Coinmarketcap.com - one of the oldest crypto price tracking sites, far more popular than Coincheckup, but offers less data;
- Blockfolio - another popular cryptocurrency tracker.

Now let's get to the good stuff.

Step 1 - Understanding your risk profile

Many people will advise you to buy "low capitalization" cryptocurrencies and tokens (i.e. between 10 and 100 million dollars) because they have a greater opportunity for growth in terms of percentage.

Although this statement is relatively correct, you have to keep in mind that the smaller a coin is, the riskier it is to invest in it. Why? Because the project has indeed a much higher risk of failing.

In traditional investments, most people aim and are happy to get an annual return of 3% - 4%; but they could be in serious financial difficulty if the invested capital is lost, so most of the time more well-known, safer and more stable titles are selected.

Other people would instead be satisfied only with an annual yield of 7% - 12%. These people could also be willing to lose all their investment if things go wrong. In their case, they would point to a higher risk given the economic attitude they have at the base.

These two different groups of people have different "risk profiles."

It is important that in any purchase you make in your life (even for something "concrete" like a car), you do so knowingly about the financial risk profile you can afford to take.

My personal opinion is that just because something has higher chances of performance does not mean it is the best choice. In particular, I have invested mainly in the top 5 coins in terms of capitalization, because they are the safest spot right now. However, I always allocate a small part of my portfolio, 10% to be precise, to low cap coins. How do I find the most promising one? Here is what I do.

Step 2 - Identification of new coins or tokens

There are three main ways I usually use to find the "new" coins or tokens:

- Through the posts of the Bitcointalk.org forum, more precisely in the section "Announcements (Altcoins)";
- In the subreddit / r / cryptocurrency;

- In the "Newly Added" sections of Coincheckup and "Recently Added" by Coinmarketcap.

Each of these is a great resource to discover interesting coins with great return potential over a shorter period of time. As already said, I only put in a maximum of 10% of my capital into these underrated projects.

With every investment comes the possibility to get scammed and in the crypto world it happens more often than I would like to see. During the last three years of experience, I have developed a series of principles that I follow in order to avoid being scammed. Here is what will make me decide NOT to invest in an asset.

Step 3 - Exclusion of coins and useless tokens/scams

One of the first things I do when I look at new projects is to subject them to very strict criteria to remove "fluff" projects from the list. In particular:

- I do not buy cryptocurrencies from industries and sectors that I do not understand;

- I do not buy cryptocurrencies whose teams are inactive in social media communication;
- I do not buy cryptocurrencies whose startups/associations/companies are registered in countries where I cannot validate a solid corporate entity;
- I do not buy cryptocurrencies if I cannot find the team members (with particular attention to the founder) on LinkedIn and validate that they are real profiles;
- I do not buy cryptocurrencies whose teams adopt spamming strategies and do aggressive and non-informative marketing campaigns on social and non-social channels;
- If a team is building a brand-new technology, I do not buy the cryptocurrency/token unless there is a detailed technical document explaining how it works;
- If a cryptocurrency has a pre-ICO with a discount, I tend not to buy it. If I did, it would only be in the case where the discount compared to the public ICO is minimal and the amount purchased is "locked" for a significant

period of time (to avoid massive dumps after the public ICO);

- I do not buy cryptocurrencies if I do not use them personally as an end user.

To help me with the process, I also use a series of questions that allow me to get more in depth and realize the true fundamental value of an asset. In particular, I really like to ask myself the following questions:

- Would I use this cryptocurrency as an end user?
- Would I pay that price as a user?
- Does this project require the development of a new technology?
- What is the team's experience in this determined direction? Have they already managed a successful company? What was the performance of this company?
- Does the team have the ability to develop this technology? Are engineers and developers recognized in this sector? Do they have product managers and customer support?

- Is it clear how the project will generate users/customers?
- Why are they using the blockchain? Do they really need it or do they use the term "blockchain" to hype their project up? What are the pros and cons of using the blockchain in this case and why should the blockchain improve the current alternative on the market? (Keep in mind that currently, in most cases, blockchain-based systems are slow and expensive).

Pay attention to absolutist statements. Each project has negative aspects and consequences; a real project will be realistic in delineating them, especially the latter.

If I can see that each question has a positive answer, I will then allocate a part of my portfolio. I always invest long term, and I am willing to stay in a coin for at least one year. If, for any reason, I do not feel confident enough to put money into a project for at least 52 weeks then that means that it is probably better to look at another one.

Predicting the next currency that will make the boom is impossible, out there one can come across so many projects based on nothing that still capitalize tens of billions of dollars; in the same way, there are dozens of serious projects that deserve more, but that fails to stand out and gain visibility compared to others. The golden rule is that which applies in every financial market: diversify. By diversifying between several coins, you reduce the risk.

Chapter 8

Technical and Fundamental Analysis

Technical Analysis is the study of graphs. Looking at the charts, the analyst is able to understand if that stock (or market) will rise or fall in a short, medium and long term. The Fundamental Analysis instead bases its forecasts on the "fundamental factors," like news, market rumors, company acquisitions, economic crises, political events, wars, etc.

Which is better between
 Technical Analysis and Fundamental Analysis? Who has never asked this question? The answer is simple; as always in investments, there is no better option

, it depends on the investor, on his way of operating in the markets, on his degree of risk, etc. In other words, there are those who are better off with one, and there are those who are better off with the other.

I personally love the Technical Analysis much more for some reasons. Let me present some of them:

- Timing: Technical Analysis offers better Timing than Fundamental Analysis. Timing is "the right time to get into a position," the ideal time to enter the market. It is, in my opinion, one of the fundamental concepts to succeed in the stock exchange. If you use the right timing you can afford a very tight Stop Loss, so you can only lose a little. So cut the losses and let the winnings run, the golden rule of the stock exchange. Timing is obviously given by the key levels that are obtained without problems with the study of the graphs, and then through Technical Analysis.
- Flexibility: Technical Analysis is more flexible than Fundamental Analysis since it gives us key

levels (for Stop Loss and Goals) in any time-frame.

- Discount: Technical Analysis discounts the Fundamental Analysis, basic postulate of Technical Analysis. The chart already includes all the factors, all the news, all the wars, all the economic conditions, etc. As a result, if the price has risen the fundamentals will be bullish. If the price has dropped the fundamentals will be bearish. I can only take care of the chart, thus eliminating many variables.

In addition to this, Fundamental Analysis has the defect that certain news is difficult to find for a common investor, and sometimes when this news arrives, it is now useless, because someone smarter than us has already used it and bought (or sold) before us.

We close with a sort of "metropolitan legend" of trading, a widespread belief (but wrong) that many still have today. Many investors believe that the Technical Analysis serves to make investments in the short term and that the Fundamental Analysis serves to make long-term investments. This is not true. Both can be used to operate in the short, medium and long term.

So many investors will continue to appreciate one and many to appreciate the other. A good idea, sometimes, is to use both, thus combining the advantages of one with the advantages of the other. An application of this concept has been explained regarding refuge currencies and high-yield currencies in Forex.

Can technical and fundamental analysis co-exist?

Although technical and fundamental analysis are considered as opposite poles, many market participants have made a winning combination. For example, some fundamental analysts use the tools of technical analysis to identify the best times to enter the market.

Nevertheless, many technical analysts exploit the economic fundamentals to support technical signals. For example, if a technical pattern on the chart indicates the possibility of selling, we can refer to the fundamental data to obtain a confirmation of this pattern.

A mix of technical and fundamental analysis is not well received by the "extremists" of both schools of thought, but the benefit we can derive from fully understanding the technical and fundamental analyst's mindset is undeniable.

Chapter 9

How to Keep Growing Your Skills

Once you have established a profitable trading strategy that generates a passive income every single month, you cannot fly to Thailand and live the laptop lifestyle just yet. As the millionaire, Dan Lok said, *just because it works, it does not mean it will last forever*. I really want this to sink in as it is one of the most important notions from the entire book.

When things are moving in the right direction, it is time to triple down on your effort and truly commit yourself to mastery. In particular, there are two things that I'd like you to do once the first profits start to come.

Create partnerships with other traders and start a business

It is true, creating friendships, alliances and partnerships is fundamental for sustainability. Having people working in your own field of interest near you can be very useful. You can exchange ideas, opinions, and advice. On the other hand, if someone thinks that this kind of alliances can be found between relatives and friends, he will find himself crashing into a wall. Friends and relatives, if not already in the sector, will be the biggest obstacle. They will be those who at every error will point their finger at you, not because they do not love you, but because the brain rejects everything that it does not understand. This is why I always suggest to work on your financial goals on your own and to share what you are doing only after getting the first sign of success. Remember that at the earlier stages your mindset is very weak and even the slightest critique can make it collapse.

Find a mentor

One of the great things about success is that it leaves footsteps: almost anything you would like to do to improve your life has already been done by someone else. It does not matter whether you are starting a business, beginning your trading journey, having a happy marriage, losing weight, quitting smoking, running a marathon or simply organizing a perfect lunch. There is certainly someone who did it very well and has left some clues.

When you are able to take advantage of these precious clues, you will discover that life is like a game in which you must connect the dots, and all the dots have already been identified and organized by others. All you have to do is follow their project and use their system.

Chapter 10

Different Trading Styles

Now that we have spent some time talking about forex trading and how to get started on it and we did all the research, it is time to work on dealing with the actual trading styles. If the currency is a good one (which you should be able to determine from the research that you did before), it is time to pick out the strategy that you are going to use in order to get started. Keep in mind that if you are going with a popular stock, the price is going to be high to start with and it can be hard to get started.

Before we look at some of the strategies that you are able to use with currencies trading, we need to remember that it is not a good idea to chase a stock. Chasing means that you will raise your buying price quickly because you are desperate to get the shares instead of someone else. This is a really bad thing to work with because your emotions are going to start running and you will often spend a lot more on the stock (and sometimes it will be a bad stock) than it is worth. Eventually, the buyers who chased the stock will find that the value of the stocks will go down and the price will go the same way, making it hard to sell them at all, even for a loss.

One thing that you should remember is that it is important to pick out a strategy that you want to work with and then stick with it. Most of the strategies that are listed below, as well as some of the others that you may find or hear about in your work, are going to help you to make a good return on investment if you learn how to use them properly and you don't skip from one strategy to another.

Some beginners find that when they make a trade, and it doesn't work while using one strategy, they will try to move over to another strategy and get this one to give them some of the results that they need. They assume that there was something wrong with that initial strategy and that they just need to try something else. The problem comes when they do this over and over again, switching strategies each time that something goes wrong.

This is an example of letting the emotions get in the way of what you want to do. If you are always switching out the strategy that you want to use, you are never really learning how to use one of them, and your whole plan is going to become a mess. You need to pick one and really get to know it, understanding how it works from all angles and in all situations, in order to get the best results with your trading. Over time you may find that it is better to get rid of one strategy and change it to another because the one isn't working or you find one will work better with your style, but it is never a good idea to skip around on the strategies that you are using all the time because it is just going to confuse you and makes it hard to ever see the success that you want with currencies.

The good news is that when you pick a strategy to work with inside of currencies, you are able to avoid the issues with chasing or some of the other issues that can come up when using currencies and trying to make a purchase. There are many strategies that you are able to pick from so you don't have to feel that you are only going to be able to use one and not feel comfortable with it. Some of the trading strategies that you may want to consider when working with currencies include:

swing trading

When it comes to working with swing trading, the investor is going to buy and then also sell their security in just one day, sometimes doing it several times during this day with at least one of their stocks. Fortunes can be made with this kind of trading, but they can also be quickly lost. In order to get the swing trading to work, you need to have a lot of experience and knowledge in your marketplace, a good strategy, and sufficient capital. You are not able to get into it at the last minute, and you must be able to think clearly to keep your losses in check.

There are a number of benefits going with swing trading including:

1. The potential profits that you can earn will be huge if you get more than one trade that is profitable during the day.

2. The risk that comes with the stock or company changing is going to be reduced because you are not holding onto the stocks for that long. It is not likely that the company is going to change in just a day.

There are also a few cons that come with the swing trading option, which is one of the reasons that people choose to go with one of the other methods of trading. Some of the cons that you will find with swing trading include:

- You need to have an account balance that is pretty large before you can even get started.
- For those who are not used to working in the stock market and who can't control their emotions well can quickly lose a lot of money.
- Since you need to use a margin account, this type of trading can make you lose more money than you put in, which can be really dangerous in this option.

Momentum Trading

The next strategy that you may want to go with is momentum trading. This is a strategy that the investor would use if the stocks are moving quickly, as well as on a high volume, going in one direction. When it comes to currencies, many of the investors are going to play on an upward momentum because these are not usually going to be available for a short sale.

Stocks that have momentum, is

 because there is some buzz that is going on around the stock, such as through the news or because of rumors. To find these stocks, you will need to do some research and read through forums, message boards, and the news to find out what is going on. You should be able to find a few stocks that are getting quite a bit of attention at a time, which means that traders are going to be playing the stock pretty hard in order to get the price to go one way, and then they will take their profit before it all goes downward again.

There needs to be some research that goes into using this option. You need to take the time to watch how the activity for trading on the stock is doing before you make the purchase. Ones that have potential to be done with momentum are ones that have a really high volume and stocks that are moving either much higher or in the opposite direction compared to the market. You will be able to watch out for these signs by looking at charts and watching the Level 2 quotes and the price action.

So after you have a list of the stocks that you would like to use, it is time to make the purchase. You will want to purchase it as quickly as possible, at as low of a price as possible, before the momentum starts to go down again. Once you own the currencies, you need to be ready to go, watching the changes in the market, looking at charts, and seeing if there are any new filings or news. If you see that there is anything negative about the stock, such as bad news, bad indicators, or a negative trend, you should try to do a quick sell to cut the lasses before moving on; this is not an industry where you wait it out to see if it gets better.

On the other hand, if the momentum keeps going up, you will still need to hold on to the stocks and wait until some of the bids start to pile up. If the momentum is going up when you receive these bids and they are high enough for you to consider, you may want to go with one of them. The momentum can quit going up at any time and could start to lower so take a bid that you are comfortable with before the tides start to turn. There may be a chance of earning more if you hold onto them longer, but if you hold on too long, you are going to lose it all so it is better to get what you can out of them.

Some of the benefits that you will be able to see with momentum trading include:

- The currencies are often going to be the ones that move the most when momentum starts to move, which means that you are able to make a lot of money in a short amount of time.
- You will be able to find a lot of information through message boards and other forums in order to pick the stocks that are right for you.

While this is a great way to make some good money in a short amount of time, there are also some cons that you will need to watch out for. Some of the cons of using momentum trading include:

- Sometimes the currencies are going to be volatile so your opportunity to sell and make a profit can be too short to earn anything.
- Companies that have dilution agendas can sometimes stall out a momentum run.
- Some people will use this idea in order to get more people to want their stocks. They will fake the buzz and the news, so you need to be careful with working with them.

Swing Trading

Another option that you are able to work with is the swing trading. This type of trading is good if you are working on a stock that has the potential to move around in a short time period. This is usually going to be for stocks that will move within the day but can go for up to four days. This is a type that will use a technical analysis in order to look for a stock that may have a momentum for their price over the short term. With this one, you are not going to be that interested in the values of the stock, but rather the trends and patterns of their price.

In a perfect market, the stocks are going to trade below or above a baseline value, or a moving average. The currencies are going to use this as both the resistance and support levels. When you are experimenting around with the charts, you will be able to see a set of moving averages which will fit to the actions of the price, and this can help out with the decisions during trading. Someone who has been in the stock market for some time would know that they should buy near the bottom of the moving average, but then they would sell before it reaches the target moving average.

There are quite a few pros that can come with this option:

- This is a good style to use for beginners who are trying to get into the market and still make some profits.

- Home runs are not usually going to be done with swing trading, but if you catch the beginning of a new uptrend, there is the possibility of getting large profits.
- You can use the basics of this kind of trading in any market that you would like. Big board stocks, futures, XCM, and Forex also use swing trading.

While there are quite a few positives that come with using currencies, there are also a few things that you need to watch out for. Swing trading is not an option that everyone is going to be fond of. Some of the cons of choosing swing trading as your strategy include:

- It is hard to find that perfect market where a particular currency is going to end up trading between the resistance and the support levels. This can get even harder to predict when there is a strong downtrend or a strong uptrend that are at work.
- currencies can make it hard to time your buys the right way, especially when dealing with dilution on the stock that you purchased.

Technical Trading

Technical trading is a good option to go for when you are looking at all the points of your trading strategy. This one is going to use a Technical Analysis in order to help you find the right stocks that you would like to trade as well as helping you to set up your entry and then exit points to reduce losses if they would occur. Someone who decides to go with this kind of trading, is going to use charts in order to examine the whole history of the stock, take the time to observe indicators that are going on, and then they will be able to identify the trends and patterns that are going on with the price.

There are a few different indicator groups that you can use in order to work with technical trading. Some of these include:

- Strength indicators: these are the indicators that are going to compare your current price to that of its history. This helps to show how weak or strong the stock will be. The Relative Strength Indicator is the most common one to use with this. Often it is shown at the top of your charts, and it will indicate any overbought as well as oversold price conditions. Many times, this can be a tip for helping you to buy and sell at the right price for a stock.

- Moving averages: these are known as MA's, and they are indicators that are going to be generated by averaging out the price levels over so much time. These can help you to see how often the movements of the stock are either below or above their averages. These are known as crossovers and can sometimes indicate breakdowns and breakouts as well, something that is important to a trader who is trying to pick out what stock they would like to work with.

- Pattern analysis: this is the evaluation of your charts in order to identify price formations, such as shapes, that come up in the history. Sometimes you are able to see wedges, triangles, cups, handles, and more for the stock you want to work with. These formations can sometimes be used to see into the future and determine if there is going to be any downward or upward movement. Market forces often cause them, but one showing up, whether it is natural or not, will affect the action of that stock.

- Range analysis: this is where you are going to use a few different things together, such as the price range and the closing and opening prices in order to figure out where your resistance and support levels are. These can help you figure out what the best purchase, as well as sell points, are and can tell you other information, such as the levels of a breakdown and breakout with the stock.

- Gap analysis: this one is going to be done when you are able to find gaps in the charts you are looking at. A gap is going to be a spot that is inside the chart which will be caused by a price at the opening that is higher than what it was at the close the previous time period. The idea behind here is that these gaps are usually going to be filled, so you will be able to use this in order to figure out the buy prices since you know that the price will go back down to fill up this gap before it goes higher.

All of these options are going to need you to use an analysis in order to figure out when to enter the market, how long to hold on to the currencies, and when to let them go in order to make the biggest profit possible while limiting your losses. There are many benefits of using this kind of strategy including:

- Many people are on the forums and the boards who will help you to learn how to use TA and will talk to you about how to identify these hot stocks.
- Inside of currencies, these technical moves can be pretty strong. This is because TA is all there really is to help you judge a stock and the way the price will move.

Of course, while many people will use this option to help them make decisions with their trading, there are a few cons that you will need to worry about. Some of these cons include:

- Bashers and pumpers can make almost all charts look like they are negative or positive, in the hopes of luring investors without experience into doing the action that they want.

- Without paying attention to some of the fundamentals, such as the news, a trade that looks good in this analysis could quickly turn around in just a few minutes, and you could lose out.
- Using a technical analysis can be hard. It is complex and hard for some people to understand how to use.

Scalping

One of the other strategies that you can use when working in currencies is known as scalping. This is when the investor is going to make several trades throughout the day in order to make some small profits on one of the stocks that really doesn't move during that day. The scalper is going to use the bid and ask spread to make this work. They will buy their shares at the big, or somewhere close to it; they can then turn around and make a small profit. This one is not going to make them a ton of money, but it is better than nothing if you plan it out right and the market isn't moving.

You are able to repeat this kind of profit a few times in order to increase your profits. While you may only make a few dollars on each trade, when you do hundreds of these, you can make a lot of money throughout the day. This is sometimes considered swing trading but be aware that all swing trading is not scalping. Sometimes this strategy will do well, but you need to be careful because most stocks are not going to stay constant and you may end up with one that goes down in value through the day.

There are a few benefits that come from using the scalping method in your trading strategy. Some of these benefits include:

- For the most part, your currencies are going to have a large spread, which helps to give you a good profit.
- currencies are sometimes going to trade sideways right after they finish with a big move

or when they are trying to break through the resistance level.

- When you purchase at the bid and then sell right away at the ask, you will still get the lowest price on your purchase, and it reduces the risk when you sell as quickly as possible before things can change.

Of course, there are a few negatives that can come up from using the scalping process for your currencies. Some of the cons of going with this method include:

- currencies can be difficult to do this with because of their anemic volume.
- This process is going to make you work against your market makers, and this makes it difficult.
- Since currencies are high risk and this option is only going to give you a small amount of profit, it may not be the best. If you want to give it a try, it isn't bad, but some people don't think the risk is worth the reward.

All of these strategies have been used when it comes to working in currencies, and it is important to figure out which method you would like to use for your needs. You can pick any of them and see some success, but you do need to be careful. You are not going to see the good results that you want if you are skipping all over the place and not sticking with a good strategy. Those who are the most successful with currencies, as well as with some of the other investment options are the ones who will pick out one strategy and stick with it. Consider some of the strategies that we talked about in this chapter and choose the one that works the best with your needs and will help you to make the biggest profit in currencies.

No matter what strategy you use, there are best practices that all experienced and successful traders observe. These are the keys that will help you succeed. These things are not just something that you read because their true essence is in doing, so be sure to apply them to your every trade. Here are the best trading practices that you should know:

Do your research

Do not simply focus on the currencies that you want to purchase. Keep in mind that the performance of stocks heavily depends upon the overall performance of the business. Therefore, you must also give attention to the company itself. How is the company doing in the market? Does it match up well against its competitors? Remember to research the currencies that you intend to purchase, as well as the company concerned.

The scope of research is, of course, a big task. This is one of the most important parts of trading. Also, find out the factors that affect a particular stock and understand them. Are these factors present at the current moment? Is there any chance that any of these influential factors appear in the future? If so, what are the consequences? The more research and knowledge that you have the better are your chances of investing in the right currencies.

Only invest the money you can afford to lose

A very common advice known to all gamblers is this: "Only play with the money you can afford to lose." This is a common advice given to gamblers. Although trading currencies may not be considered gambling, especially if you do not rely on pure luck, it is still similar to gambling in the sense that there is always the possibility to lose your money. Do not use the money that you need for your child's enrollment or for paying the household bills, etc. Although there is no assurance that you will lose your money, you must only invest the money that you can afford to lose. The forex market is very volatile that it is hard to guarantee that you will make a profit.

Set a limit

It is a sound advice, especially for beginners, to decide before making any trade on a limit on how long will you continue to hold on to a losing stock, as well as for a profitable one. The forex market is extremely volatile. Although you can expect for their value to increase and decrease almost randomly, it does not always mean that a stock whose price has just decreased will soon increase.

Part of the volatility of currencies is that another big drop can still follow a significant decrease in value. Therefore, in order to cut down your losses, it is important to set a limit on how long you would be willing to hold on to a losing stock. In the same way, you should know how long you will hold on to a winning stock. Again, even if a stock continuously experiences an increase in value, there is still the possibility that its price can just drop dramatically, almost without any warning.

Look for patterns

The movement of the prices of currencies can be said to be like random. The thing is, randomness creates patterns. And, if it is not random, then there is more possibility to find a pattern. If you can identify these patterns early, then you will be one step ahead. Just remember, though, that patterns are like trends; and in the world of currencies, they do not last for very long.

Observe the trends

Analyze the graphs and tables that show the performance of certain currencies. Do not just study their current record, but also check their past performance. This is a good way for you to know if the stocks are really doing well or not. Also, do not rely completely on the latest trends. Although the latest trends can show you the most recent performances of currencies, you must take note that trends often change. In fact, in the forex market, you will barely see a trend that will last for too long.

Know the latest news

If you are serious about trading currencies, then you should be updated on the latest news. The many factors that affect the prices of currencies are usually revealed on the news. Although the news would not state it directly, you should know that laws, businesses, economy, market behavior, and inflation, among others, can affect the prices of currencies. Take note, however, that although the news can give you valuable insights and information, what matters the most is still the actual prices of forex.

Stay calm

Bad days do happen, and you may encounter a series of losing streaks despite doing some good research. During such a moment, or the moment when you first experience your first loss, stay calm. I repeat: stay calm. The forex market does not care about how you feel, so you must remain objective and focused. If you cannot control yourself, just quickly turn off your computer or mobile phone.

Do not be greedy

Especially for beginners, it is recommended that you stick to getting small yet regular profits. Many inexperienced traders lose their money not because of buying the wrong forex, but because of keeping the stocks for too long. Do not underestimate the highly volatile nature of the forex market. Learn to sell, cash out, and enjoy your profit.

Keep your emotion under control

Do not be an emotional trader. Although it is good to feel passionate about trading forex, do not let your passion blind your judgment. Never make any trade when under pressure and treat trading forex as a business.

Make your own decision

Although it is advisable to read the opinions of "experts," it is wrong to let them dictate your investment decisions. Unfortunately, many of these so-called "experts" are hacks and frauds. They promote themselves as an expert even if their overall losses outweigh their profits. Of course, there are still a few real experts out there, but even the best traders still commit mistakes from time to time. After all, the process of developing your trading strategy is a life-long journey.

Instead of relying on expert advice, you should develop your own understanding of the forex market and make your own decisions. You can compare your decisions with the pieces of advice given by "experts" and see how well you match up. Of course, you also need to check the real outcome of a particular trade to see if you have made the right investment decision.

Do not chase after your losses

This is another advice given to gamblers. Unfortunately, although this advice is very common, many still fail to observe it. There are several ways to chase after your losses, but they all usually lead to the same unfortunate result. Usually, you chase after your losses by investing more right after you lose a trade. When you lose, you simply have this strong urge to get your money back.

Another thing people do is by continuously holding on to losing stocks, thinking that once they sell them, they would no longer save their lost investment. In any way, you are on the losing side with just a little hope of getting your losses back. The bad thing here is that you gamble your whole funds for the sake of recovering a few losses. Therefore, the risk is really high.

A good way to avoid this is by learning to accept your losses. If certain currencies fail to meet your expectations, learn to accept your losses by selling them and starting over again. When you seriously engage in trading forex, losing some investments is normal. After all, once you get lucky and hit truly profitable stocks, you will quickly recover all your losses and enjoy grand profits.

Stick to your strategy

During the execution process, you must do your best to stick to your planned strategy; otherwise, you will not be able to measure effectiveness, as well as its full potential. Of course, there are instances that you should abandon your strategy, especially if circumstances clearly show that continuing with your strategy will result in a total loss of investment.

Only invest in currencies that have a high volume

According to some "expert," you should only invest in stocks that trade at least a hundred thousand shares per day. This serves as a safeguard against the risk of being illiquid.

Pump your currencies

There is a reason why the pump and dump scheme still exists despite many people being aware of such a scheme: It works.

So, if you do not mind being a bit tricky, you can market yourself as an "expert" in trading currencies. You can put up a website and send out newsletters to your readers. You can then purchase cheap currencies, use your connections to gain interest in the stocks, and sell them at a premium price. If you are the type that can convince people to do what you want, then this may be an easy way for you to make money. However, if you are the type who cannot exercise a bit of trickery (which is a very good thing about you), then you can simply take advantage of people who pump and dump their stocks. How? Simply buy their currencies, preferably before they pump them or as early as possible while they pump their value. You can then wait for their price to increase, sell your currencies, and reap some profits.

Keep a journal

Writing a journal is not required, but it is very helpful. You do not have to be a professional writer to write a journal. What is important is for you to be honest about everything that you write.

There are many things that you can write in your journal. It is also good to write your goals and reasons why you want to trade forex. Also, write any lessons and mistakes that you have learned. It is your journal, so feel free to write about anything and everything about your trading adventure. A journal will allow you to think outside the box and be a smarter trader.

Take a break

Trading forex has a gambling factor: It can be addicting. It is something that you can do for hours without being tired. You would feel more like playing than working. However, when you engage in research, which is a must, that is the time where you will definitely feel that trading forex involve serious work. Allow yourself to take a break from to time. Remember that you will have better mental clarity if you give yourself a chance to take a rest.

Get the latest updates quickly

Successful traders get the latest news and respond quickly. The way to take advantage of the impact of the news on the prices of stocks is by making the appropriate trading actions just before others realize them. For example, when you see that your currencies will soon encounter a massive drop in value, sell them right away. Also, if possible, know the news before it is even released to the public to increase the probability that certain stocks will increase in value, the stocks should also be effectively promoted. Therefore, it is helpful if you can join and be active in online groups and forums on forex trading.

Focus on the main pairs

One of the best things about the forex market is that it is a place where you can find many start-up companies. Surely, a good number of these companies will do well. Unfortunately, some of them will perform badly and even get bankrupt. However, if you manage to get the stocks of the good start-up companies early on, you will find yourself in a winning position.

Therefore, you must exert the effort to research and analyze the different start-up companies that participate in the forex market. When analyzing a particular company, also measure how it matches up against its competitors in the market.

Growing companies have lots of space for improvements; and as their profits increase and they continue to expand, the prices of their currencies also increase.

Have fun

It is a common advice that you should choose a job that you enjoy. In the same way, you should enjoy trading forex. If you do not enjoy it, then maybe it is a signal that you should just invest somewhere else. Also, you can make better decisions when you are having fun.

Choose the right currencies

Always choose the right currencies to invest in. How do you know the right ones? Sufficient research. Never commence a trade without sufficient research. Take note that a little research is not enough. Researches made without serious efforts are only as good as a mere toss of a coin. Also, the most profitable and attractive-looking stocks may not always be the right currencies to invest in. After all, no matter what the media says, the numbers on the forex market are what counts.

Be patient

Patience is important when you trade currencies. Do not hurry to make a buy order simply because you have funds in your account. Also, many times, to take advantage of the high volatility of forex trading, you will have to wait for some time. Take note that every action that you make is essential. The stocks that you buy today are the stocks that you will soon sell. Be patient, wait for the proper timing, and act accordingly.

Use the high volatility to your advantage

Although many people shy away from forex trading due to its high volatility, it is this volatile nature of forex that makes them a profitable investment. With high volatility, mastering the famous principle for making money is the key to profit: buy when the price is low, and sell when the price is high.

Chapter 11

A Few Important Notes

As a beginner, you may be a bit worried about getting started with forex trading. These are going to take a different route compared to working with traditional stock market options and sometimes it is hard to find the information that you need about the company before making the investment that you want. With that being said, it is possible to be successful when using currencies; you just need to be careful with the decisions that you make in currencies and take your time to really see results. Some of the tips that you can follow when you get started with currencies to help you be successful include:

Ignore some of the success stories

When you first get started with currencies, you are going to get a lot of information and emails about the success stories of others who have done well with currencies. These are found in social media sites and emails, but often these are unusual circumstances, or the information is all made up.

Instead of focusing on this, you need to look at the stocks on their own and see if they are going to work for you. Just ignore all of the success stories since most of these are going to be in order to get you to make a certain purchase. Do your research and learn about the market to determine which ones are the right ones for you.

Read through the disclaimers

If you are receiving a newsletter about the currencies, you need to be careful about the tips that you are reading. There is nothing wrong with picking out some of the stocks from these options, but you should be aware that most of them are sales tips and to give exposure to companies that, for the most part, are really bad and could end up making you lose a lot of money.

Most of the newsletters that you are going to pick won't give you the full story. The people who are writing them will do so in order to pump out the stock, and they are not going to tell you the right time to sell the stocks. They will work hard to get you to purchase their stocks, and then you never hear from them again. It is fine to read through some of these to get some information, but when the disclaimers state that these are written as a promotion for one company or another, you know that the tips are more of a sales pitch rather than as good advice.

Sell quickly

One of the allures that you will hear about with currencies is that you are able to get a huge return on investment, up to 30 percent, in just a short amount of time. If you want to make a return on investments like this with currencies, you will need to sell your stocks quickly after you purchase them. Unfortunately, instead of being happy with the 30 percent or so, people will get greedy and will look to make a huge return. Considering currencies are sometimes getting pumped out, and the industry is volatile, you should be happy with what you get, or you may lose out on a lot of money.

Be careful when listening to the fund management

You need to be really careful about the people you are listening to inside of currencies trading, even when it comes to fund management of the stock currencies you are working with. These companies are trying to work in order to get the stocks up. When the stock's up, these companies are able to raise more money, and it is more likely they will stay in business. In some instances, they may not even be companies, but basically, insiders who are trying to get rich.

In fact, most of the promotions that you will see come from the same group of people who will use different companies and press releases in order to get some hype up and make some extra money. They may have purchased the stocks at a lower price and now want to create a lot of buzz to get you to make a purchase much higher than what they paid.

In between the people who are using pump and dump to make money and the companies who are worried about going under and want to get you to agree with them to save them from failing, it is hard to know which currencies are safe. You need to think independent of the news and some of the promotions that you hear before picking out the stocks that you want to invest in. With some good research and being critical of things you hear, it is easier to pick out the currencies that are actually good and to make the money you want.

Focus on high volume

When you are getting started, it is best only to use stocks that have a minimum of 100,000 shares traded each day. If you go with a stock that is too low in volume, it is sometimes too hard to get yourself out of this issue. In addition, experts recommend that you pick out the stocks that are selling for over 50 cents a share. Going with stocks that are lower in price than this may seem appealing, but often these aren't considered liquid enough to really play with. But if you pick out stocks that are getting more than 100,000 shares a day traded and they are over 50 cents for each share, you are going to have more luck getting them to sell nicely.

Pick the best stock out of the bunch

You should make sure that you pick out one of the best stocks that you can find, especially when you are a beginner in this industry. Some experts recommend that you find a stock that has really good earnings overall or one that has broken out of its average 52-week highs in volume. Some of these are easy to find, but the trick with these is that you want to find ones that have these highs, but not because of a pump and dump scheme. You want the highs to be because others are interested in the stock and the value is going up naturally, not because of some buzz that is created to inflate the price.

Chapter 12

Chart Analysis

Indicators and charts are one of the most important components when we talk about technical analysis. In addition to experience, coldness, and psychology, a good analyst cannot disregard a thorough knowledge of the graphs. The latter can represent different information and may appear in different forms.

In graphical analysis, the graphs deserve particular attention because they represent the price dynamics of a given financial instrument and in a given period.

In the technical analysis, the most commonly used type of graph is certainly the candlestick chart, better known under the name of a Japanese candlestick chart. Before moving on to a detailed description of the candlestick chart, however, I would like to say a few words about two other charts, less used than candlestick charts, but which may be useful as they can help you understand the Japanese candlestick chart.

The price chart is shown on a Cartesian plane where, on the abscissa axis, that is the vertical axis the time is reported, while on the horizontal axis the price is reported.

Given this premise, we can still say that the graphs refer to different time periods whether they are fractions of minutes, hours and days, if not even weeks, months or even years indicating different sizes of opening or closing, of maximums and minima.

On the axis of the abscissas, we find a space called histogram of the volume, which represents the quantity of instruments exchanged during the period under examination.

In graphic analysis in the specific and more generally in the technical analysis, various types of graph are used.

Features of a good chart

With the above, I do not mean that you will need a chart that contains a myriad of information or detailed information in detail, but I would like to emphasize that the best successful traders on the market, use very few indicators. Yes, you understood correctly. Only a few indicators. You will, therefore, think that what has been described up to now is only a chat, but it is not so, as these extrapolate the most important information directly from the graph. The charts obviously can only be provided by the brokers, which as for the forex market, here too we advise you to always choose the best binary options brokers. So it is not true that the graphics are all the same, it will be the good broker to extrapolate all the information that interests him from the various detailed charts. And from here we recognize the best brokers.

The reason for this extrapolation is very simple: since the indicators express only the past in a graphic form, they can provide a very approximate vision of the future. So too many indicators in a chart can sometimes create confusion instead of aid.

Therefore, we consider very important to keep the following points in mind:

- Good graphic program.

With this, in fact, you should always be able to look far enough in the past, to plan the future and identify relevant barriers and gather a satisfactory overview. In the binary options charts of the different brokers, this time frame is too narrow to draw reliable conclusions.

- Good quality graphs always indicate different time intervals.

These range from a few minutes to a max. of a month.

- Never set just a common linear chart.

This fact would not be very useful for technical analysis purposes. On the other hand, candle or beam charts are used, which we will explain briefly.

What is chart analysis?

The analysis of the graphs is above all the search for particular shapes, also called graphic structures, configurations, figures.

They are figures that emerge from the price movement, and that can signal its future trend. They are tracked by analysts joining points in the price graph of a financial security or the performance of an indicator.

The purpose of the graphic analysis will, therefore, be to identify the most typical price patterns for forecasting purposes.

These graphic formations can be classified into different categories. The main categories of classes can assume inversion or continuation or consolidation characteristics. Fundamental features will also be the dynamics of the volumes, which we will explain under each figure.

This is why it takes technique, experience, strategies, if not the analyst's ability to see these forms in the movement of a graph. These are the fundamental elements of this type of analysis. The concept of trendline, support and resistance are also part of this aspect of technical analysis.

Below we will list the most used graphs for graphic analysis and explain the operation. Before doing this, however, we must explain another very important and used concept: the figure of Continuation. These have common characteristics in all the graphs, they represent a pause in the prevailing trend in progress and are a prelude to a continuation of the trend in the direction of the direction previously underway. For this reason, they are also known as consolidation figures.

The main difference between the continuation and the inversion figures concerns the extension.

The continuation figures are often accompanied by a decrease in the volumes traded.
One of the first figures we are going to examine is the wedge.

Wedge

This too is a continuation figure on explained and is very similar to the triangle for 2 reasons:

- for the form;
- For the time it takes to form. This differs from the triangle that we will see below because the shape that forms is characterized by a strongly bullish or bearish inclination opposite to that of the current trend.

This means that:

- this chart consists of two convergent trendlines and takes about one to three months to develop;
- in an uptrend, a falling wedge or "a descending wedge" can be encountered;
- while in a bearish tendency a rising wedge or "an ascending wedge" can develop.

As with the pennant and flag figures, the wedge can be found in the middle of a movement, thus allowing to calculate minimum targets.

The dynamics of the volumes see a decrease in the course of the formation of the pattern and it should go to be reduced for all the period of formation of the figure. On the contrary, they increase significantly when the trendline is broken, which is a typical feature of the wedge.

The second figure we examine in this chapter is the pennant.

Pennant

This figure is also quite common in chart analysis.

This figure together with the figure of the flag, which we will see immediately after the flag appears after an almost vertical movement and represents a pause in the trend.

Its characteristic is that it is presented as a symmetrical triangle which, however, has a maximum extension of 3 weeks. Most often, in bearish actions, the refinement time of the figure is even lower and is equal to one or maximum two weeks. The pennant is halfway to the bullish or bearish movement, with the obvious implications in calculating the minimum targets for the movement's arrival.

It will, therefore, be obvious that the volume decreases during the formation of the figure and should be low throughout the period of formation of the pattern. On the contrary, instead, they increase significantly when the trendline breaks, which identifies the pennant. These are accompanied by a similar trend in the range within which prices move.

Pennants, most often coincide with a contraction phase, which does not necessarily have an opposite inclination with respect to the basic trend.

Both this figure and the next develop within a rather short time frame.

The third figure that we examine as announced is the Flag.

Flag

Flag formation, or flag, is a very common pattern of continuation in graphic analysis.

This form tends to appear close to the temporary exhaustion of a trend, which represents a brief pause in the market after strongly accentuated movements, are almost vertical and known as flagpole.

The flag has a shape similar to a parallelepiped, almost to represent a rectangle, bounded by two parallel trendlines but opposed to the prevailing trend. In other words, it can be seen as a flag that is tilted downward in an uptrend and upward in a bearish trend.

His training ends within a medium period, that is between one and three weeks. It usually appears halfway to complete movement.

It must also be said that if it is in a bearish movement the perfection time is less and the figure is usually completed in one or two weeks. Precisely because it is in the middle of the bullish or bearish movement, the figure is important for identifying price targets. From here we will then calculate the width of the movement preceding the flag and report this distance after the break of the trendline delineating the figure.

The volume should also decrease during the formation of the figure and then increase again when the trendline is broken.

So let's see how to use Flag and Pennant.

The targets that can be identified in relation to these figures are two:

- The first is determined by projecting the width of the base from the breakout point; here this target assumes less importance if we consider the reduced dimensions of the figure.
- The second can instead be obtained by projecting, from the breakout point, a distance equivalent to that covered by the movement that preceded the formation of the pennant.

- This means that these figures often materialize around half of the overall movement, giving a fair advantage at the operational level.

The temporary phase of price weakness can be exploited to enter the stock or even just to increase the position taken earlier, again using a stop-loss much lower than the potential take-profit.

The rectangle will represent the fourth figure that we will explain.

Rectangle

The rectangle is the simplest among the figures proposed by the technical analysis.

It identifies a phase of price congestion. In Technical Analysis, with this term, we mean a graphic formation in correspondence with which prices oscillate within a narrow range of values. This process takes place when the market moves sideways.

The pattern represents a break zone of the current trend in which prices move sideways. This also gives rise to the name of trading range or congestion area, a figure that represents a period of consolidation of the current trend that is resolved in the direction of the trend that preceded it. This represents a fundamental figure, to correctly identify the continuation pattern if not also the observation of the volumes.

Also, for this bullish figure, the rebounds must be accompanied by high volumes, with the corrections characterized by decreasing volumes. In the opposite case, instead, in the bearish rectangle, are the corrections to have more accentuated volumes.

Many investors, take advantage of the oscillations, selling to the top of the figure and buying at the minimum. However, those who use this approach risk not exploiting the breaking of the pattern.

The figure in question usually takes from one to three months to improve, and the minimum target is represented by the translation of the height of the rectangle when the price breaks the figure.

Prices move within a fixed band identified by a support and resistance.

The rectangles can also be configured as inversion figures, depending on the context in which they are formed. It is therefore evident how the congestion phases identify a moment in which the market expresses considerable uncertainty and awaits new information to decide the future trend. Unlike the contraction phases (in which the continuous reduction in volatility identifies in an increasingly precise manner the moment in which the market will receive the information that awaits) a figure of congestion like the rectangle does not allow to identify sufficiently in advance the moment in which the breakout will take place.

The operational cues that this figure can provide are basically of two types:

- The first requires waiting for the exit of prices from the congestion zone initially identified. This exit must necessarily be classified as a breakout and therefore must be characterized by an increase in volumes and volatility.

- The second operational step derives from the possibility of exploiting the lateral movement of prices to buy close to the identified support and sell when the values are near the top of the figure again.

Support and Resistance

Let me now explain briefly what are the supports and the resistance.

Support is defined as that price level at which there is, an arrest of the downward trend in prices. An excessive concentration of purchases that occurs in the vicinity of the same will cause a block in the downward trend in prices.

A level of support is defined as reliable when it shows resistance to repeated "attacks" without a bearish breakdown.

The Resistance is defined instead as that level of price where the growth of the same stops. In the case of the

Resistance, the high concentration of sales prevents the continuation of the increase.

A resistance level, on the contrary, is stronger and more reliable as it resists repeated "attacks" without an upward failure.

Surely a historical minimum or maximum represents a level of Support or Strategic Resistance.

Consequently, the penetration or breaking of support levels or even resistance can be caused by:

- important changes in the fundamental values of a company (increase in profits, changes in management, etc.);
- from simple forecasts based on price trends in recent times;
- both levels of support and resistance can also arise from motivations exclusively of an emotional nature. Supports and resistances represent with great simplicity the encounter/clash between supply and demand.

From the above it is clear that in practice, a breakout, or an event in which the price comes out of a trend, breaking a support or resistance or a channel, above a level of resistance evidence an increase in demand, arising from more buyers, who are willing to buy at higher prices than the current ones.

In the opposite case, instead, the breakdown of a support shows an increase in the sellers, and therefore in the offer, as more sellers are willing to sell even at lower prices than the current ones.

If a level of support is broken, it automatically turns into a resistance level, just as if a resistance level is broken, it becomes a level of support. This process is known as pullback, which is a time when a trending market takes a break.

The support and resistance lines can be drawn horizontally and then we will talk about static support, where the support corresponds to a precise and constant point in time; both obliquely and in this case, we will talk about dynamic support, where a trendline is drawn with the variation of prices and with the passage of time.

The fifth figure, object of study concerns the triangle.

Triangle

In technical analysis, that of the triangle is a consolidation figure and is used to verify the continuation of the main trend. This is a pattern that lasts a few months when there is a pause in the current trend with prices that oscillate in an increasingly narrow area.

The figure has the following characteristics:

The triangle must have a minimum of four reaction points; two superiors, and two inferior; the first ones necessary to trace the upper trendline, the seconds necessary to draw the lower trend line.

A time limit for its resolution characterizes the triangle. Usually, the prices break the triangle at a point between two-thirds and three-quarters of the depth of the triangle.

The volumes in the formation phase of the triangle waves, lose strength and then explode when the trendline that delimits the figure breaks.

The minimum target for price trends is calculated by projecting the maximum height of the triangle.

The figure in question can present itself according to three different structures:

symmetrical triangle which has the trendlines that delimit it that are convergent.
Prices tend to move in a range that gradually becomes narrower with the passing of the sessions, due to a constant reduction of the maximums, and also due to a constant reduction of the minimums.

A descending triangle characterized by a flat demarcation line, the lower one, and by a bearish trend line, the upper one.

In this figure, there will be a greater conviction on the part of the bearish and is often found during a downward trend.

The reduction in the range within which prices move, occurs only thanks to an increase in the minimum, while the maximums remain almost unchanged.

Just such behavior makes evident the greater pressure of the buyers with respect to the sellers and attributes to this figure a bullish value.

Descending triangle
The figure represents a symmetrical structure, which makes it difficult to interpret. In the third case, on the other hand, we speak of an ascending triangle, characterized by an upper line of flat demarcation and a line, the lower, ascending line. This pattern indicates a greater strength of the uptrend and is often found during an uptrend
Regardless of the configuration, whether symmetrical, ascending or descending, it is possible to calculate the target of the figure, i.e., the level that prices should reach in the phase following the breakout.

This is calculated by projecting, from the breaking point, the "base" of the triangle, i.e., the maximum width that the figure recorded during its formation.

The sixth figure in question concerns the formation of broadening.

Broadening

This represents a rather rare figure, classified as a variant of the triangle but which presents a contrary opening, with divergent trendlines. It is a figure that occurs at the end of a trend, usually bullish.

The dynamics of the volumes are different from that of the triangles, as the volume gradually expands together with the increase in price oscillation.

The seventh figure that we are going to examine concerns the diamond.

Diamond

Also, the diamond as an inversion figure is one of the rarest and one of the least simple to detect. Graphically the diamond is formed by a double-figure composed of a first half that recalls the shape of a broadening from a second half that resembles a symmetrical triangle.

A diamond can present itself in two circumstances:

- at the end of an uptrend;
- at the end of a bearish trend;

In the first case, it takes the name of "Diamond Top," vice versa we would be facing a "Diamond Bottom."

The figure does not always develop symmetrically. Often, the second half is prolonged in time more than the first one did.

By its nature, the diamond needs very dynamic market phases. The figure of the Diamond can also occur during simple breaks of the trend.

For this reason, it is easier to find the diamond at the peak of an upward trend before a bearish reversal rather than the other way around.

The dynamics of volumes go hand in hand with that of prices. That is, if volumes increase, prices increase, in the second half. However, prices fall and consequently also volumes.

There are 4 basic elements to identify the training:

- an initial phase of price expansion;
- a maximum;
- a minimum;
- a phase of price contraction;

The pattern is only complete when the support or resistance line breaks and a pullback to the violated trendline does not always occur.

The minimum price target is equal to the maximum vertical distance between the two extreme parts of the figure projected at the bottom (or at the top) with respect to the breaking point of the support or resistance.

It is possible, even for the diamond, to calculate a target price.

It is sufficient to project the maximum width of the figure and project it starting from the point where the breakout occurred.

In the event that it is configured as a continuation figure, it is also possible to derive a second target, projecting the width of the movement that preceded the beginning of the diamond, from the point of the final breakout. Diamond breaking points.

The eighth figure we examine will be a figure difficult enough to examine and represents the rounding and spike.

Spike

This represents one of the many figures of inversions, which presents itself as a slow and gradual movement on the lows that will first have a slight downward, then lateral and then shows a growing movement.

The pattern is one of the slowest of all the graphic analysis and is usually identifiable on longer-term charts.

It is really difficult to establish the precise moment in which the figure can be considered complete, if not after the first substantial rises. More difficult, it will be to identify upward targets.

Spike is also very special. The figures in question show, without any transition period, a sudden reversal of the quotations. An inversion accompanied by an explosion of volumes.

Due to its characteristics, the figure in question is difficult to identify in advance.

Double Top and Double Bottom

Also, this falls into the categories of the inversion figures, which we remember are particular graphic figures that announce an inversion of the current trend. The figure in question turns out to be a very common figure in graphic analysis and together with other figures, the double bottom and double top figures are among the most common and recognizable formations.

We explain briefly in two essential steps, its operation;

1. The double minimum is at the peak of a bearish trend and is configured as a minimum, a subsequent rebound and a subsequent fallback to the level of the previous minimum. The ascent that follows, if it breaks on the upside and with volumes, the previous maximum, leads to the completion of the figure. The pattern, due to its shape, is also called a formation in W. Volumes are growing during the formation of the first minimum, down in the following rebound, and then increase again during the upward movement that completes the figure.

Basically, therefore, the double minimum is realized, following a clear bearish trend, in which prices test twice a price threshold, but without being able to overcome it. This determines the realization of two minimums slightly spaced over time. Double minimum and double maximum.

2. Also, the characteristics of the double maximum are the same, but the pattern has a secularly opposite development. The double top is at the height of an uptrend and is configured as a maximum, a consequent fall and a

subsequent rebound towards the previous maximum.

The double maximum is achieved when, following a sharp uptrend, prices test twice a price threshold, but without being able to overcome it, determining the formation of two maximums. Volumes are growing at the formation of the first rise, remaining lower in the formation of the second maximum and then increasing conspicuously at the time of the piercing of the traceable line starting from the previous minimum.

In both figures, it is possible to observe a return of prices to the level of completion of the pattern, in a pullback similar to that of the head and shoulders that we will see later, before the definitive start of the new trend, bullish in the double minimum and bearish in the double maximum. Small volumes accompany this pullback.

The measurement of the minimum upward (or downward) target is calculated by calculating the distance between the line joining the two minima (or the two maxima) and the first maximum (or minimum) relative and projecting this value from the upward drilling point or downward.

In essence, the double minimum or the double maximum is, however, a graphic formation with a degree of reliability lower than other figures of inversion, both because it is not always detectable with sufficient certainty, and because it often occurs in conditions of volatility so high that allow identification of a valid breakout.

Triple Top and Triple Bottom

The triple maximum and the triple minimum are also inversion figures, defined as variants of the head and shoulders, but unlike the previous ones, the three maxima and the three minima are all placed at the same height.

The volumes to be considered, in the triple minimum correspond to each rise, starting from a minimum is accompanied by decreasing volumes. The pattern is completed when the line obtained by joining the last maximum with extremely high volumes is breached upwards. triple maximum

In the triple maximum, any downward correction starting from a maximum is accompanied by declining volumes, and consequently, the figure can be said to be complete when the level obtained by joining the last lows is violated downwards with volumes in great growth. In the triple minimum, however, the minimum target is common to that used for head and shoulders, a figure that we will see shortly if not also equal to double minimum and double maximum, based on the height of the figure.

Head and Shoulders

This is also an inversion figure and is one of the most reliable graphic patterns. According to some authors, the figure in question is the most powerful among all those found on a chart.

The graph, head, and shoulders is presented, as can be deduced from the graph below, consisting of three consecutive increases, interspersed with two bearish inversions. The second rise is generally more robust than the others and represents the head, the first and third instead represent the shoulders and are less pronounced than the head. The completion of the figure is obtained by perforating the line, joining the two reaction minima, called Neck-line. The logic that underlies the formation is simple. The price cannot confirm its strength, it does not create new highs, and the trend deteriorates. The succession of rising highs and lows, a fundamental dynamic to define an uptrend, is conditioned.

During the first phase, there is the formation of a maximum accompanied by volatility and high volumes. After partial retracement prices make a new maximum, however, registering a reduction in volumes. After a new retracement, the prices make a new relative maximum, lower than the previous one and accompanied by reduced volumes. The completion of the figure requires the breakout of the neckline, which coincides with the straight line that unites the two points in which the prices have partially retraced (2 and 4). At the breakout, the volatility and volumes return to be high. The breakout moment can then be followed by a pullback, that is a price return movement close to the neckline (which, in this phase, will assume the role of resistance).

The line that joins the base formed by the two reaction minima is fundamental. This line is also called "neckline," and its importance derives from the fact that the figure is completed only when the price drills this level downwards.

The neckline is usually horizontal or inclined in the same direction as the trend to be reversed. In this last case, it has greater value.

Usually, after the neckline is broken, there is a movement of prices returning towards the neckline itself, in a dynamic called "pullback." If the prices fail to return above the neckline, confirmation of the perfection of the figure is complete.

Operationally it is possible to close the long positions at the rupture of the uptrend trendline that unites the upward minimums on the downside of the head but before opening any short positions a sharp break of the neckline is expected.

The "head and shoulders" can be configured both as a bearish figure and as a bullish figure: in the second case the three maxima described above will be replaced by three minimums, but the evolution of the figure - also from the point of view of volumes and volatility - it will remain the same. The target can be calculated by projecting the width of the figure (coinciding with the distance between the "head" and the neckline) from the breakout point. Among the inversion figures, the "head and shoulders" is perhaps the one that - once completed - provides the greatest degree of reliability, determining the achievement of the target in a rather short time, generally lower than that in which the FIG.

In the development of a head and shoulders, the dynamics of the volumes is a fundamental aspect. The three maxima, the left shoulder, the head, and the right shoulder, must have low volumes. To give a stronger confirmation to the perfection of the figure the neckline rupture should instead occur with volumes in explosion, while those of the possible pullback should be again decreasing with an increase in the subsequent downward movement.

The reputation of the head and shoulders is also due to its ability to give the chart analyst precise price targets, a feature that allows to know already at the time of entry into position which will be the likely gains of the operation but also what will be the related risks. The stop losses necessary to defend their investments can also be positioned.

We, therefore, see that the first minimum target is given by the downward projection of the calculable distance between the neckline and the vertex of the head while the second target is obtained by adding to the first target the extension of the right shoulder.

The head and shoulder variant is the inverted shoulder head, a powerful inversion figure that can be found on the market minimums and at the end of a bearish or bullish trend. The figure in question is formed by three consecutive minima, where the second minimum is more extensive than the first and third. Also, in this case, the current trend deteriorates between the head and the right shoulder.

The result is a lack of the main characteristic of a bearish tendency, that is, that of the alternation between lower and higher declines.

Traders and investors in the stock market use different techniques to choose the securities to invest in. Some make greater use of technical analysis, others of fundamental analysis.
To choose the stock to invest in, especially if you intend to do it for a medium-long period, it is good to use both types of analysis.

The fundamental analysis makes it possible to evaluate a stock, thus understanding the real underlying value of the action. Technical analysis, on the other hand, allows us to understand which are the best entry and exit points from a stock and often reflects the evaluation of the fundamental analysis.
Furthermore, by combining the two types of market analysis, one can not only analyze the graphs but also study the historical trend of an investment.
It is, in fact, important to know both the price trend at the time when you are trading, and understand the changes in the past.

In this chapter, we illustrate the fundamental analysis parameters to be taken into account when choosing a stock and you will see how technical analysis can help you climb up or down the price of an action.
Here's how to choose a stock to invest in.

As anticipated, it is preferable, in the stock market, to use both analyzes, because together they provide a clearer picture for the choice of a stock.
Starting from the fundamental analysis, the parameters on which to base for the choice of a title are the following:

- ROE and ROA (or ROI)
- the price/earnings ratio (P / E) and EPS (earnings per share)
- the price/value ratio of the book (P / BV)
- news, management quality and visibility of the title.

Let's look at each of these aspects in detail, so as to create a complete content that can guide even the less experienced in choosing actions.

The stock exchange operator who compares with the stock market to choose a stock initially looks to ROE (Return on Equity). This financial indicator offers the trader the opportunity to evaluate the rate of return on equity, i.e., the part of the financial statements that remunerates shareholders.

High levels of ROE, both current and future, indicate that the company issuing the security is able to guarantee a high return for investors.

However, the only use of ROE can be misleading as it does not take into account the level of indebtedness. By definition, equity is the difference between total assets and liabilities.

If liabilities rise, the denominator of the ROE will tend to decrease, pushing the overall value upwards. Operators then typically compare ROE with ROA (Return on Assets) which tells us how profitable the company's assets are.

High ROE and ROA values indicate that the ROE growth is truthful as the [ROA] takes into account the liabilities in the denominator that as the number increases, it will tend to increase, thus compressing the percentage of ROA.

The P / E and the EPS

Together with the ROE and the ROA, we also look at the P / E and the EPS. The P / E is the ratio between the stock price and EPS, i.e., the profit generated by the company for each outstanding share.

The P / E falls into the category of "comparables," those parameters that can be compared with those of similar or sector companies. Some operators tend to compare the P / E of a company with that of the sector, but making a mistake.

In fact, we cannot compare the P / E with the simple mathematical average of the reference sector, since the latter includes P / E of companies which, by structure and profitability, are not similar to that analyzed.

It is therefore good to compare the P / E with that of similar companies rather than the average sector. So when you do your analysis, be careful not to fall into this trap.

The EPS instead is the denominator of the P / E. If the P / E falls while the EPS rises is the ideal situation (assuming that ROE and ROA are optimal).

This is because it indicates that the share price is not reflecting earnings growth, thus showing an underestimation of the market on the security in question.

The P / BV

To give further proof of the goodness of the analysis, the P / BV intervenes (price/book value). If the ROE grows structurally well (i.e. that there are no deviations caused by the increase in debt) and the P / BV is low there is a further suggestion of underestimating the stock to be chosen.

This is because the price is not absorbing the growth of the book value (equity) which is the part of the balance sheet that interests the stock investor.

The scheme to choose

To summarize, then, the fundamental analysis formula that allows the optimal choice of a stock is:

- Current and prospective high ROE and ROA;

- P / E relatively low compared to competitors and EPS growing;
- Low P / BV (also comparable with sector competitors)

News impact

Another point that concludes the fundamental analysis of a stock is the news circulating on the issuing company and the market sentiment towards management. If we choose to invest in a stock, it is good to take a look at recent company news.

Positive news generally reflects the sentiment of the market in the company, which is a good sign for future increases in the security in question. Evaluating management skills is also a good idea because if the market positively perceives the leaders of the company, this will have a positive attitude towards the choices of managers and especially towards the stock.

Finally, consider where the stock is listed. If we are talking about small-cap companies, in phases of the market that are not at risk, the title cannot be higher. This is because the shares listed on smaller indices enjoy less visibility because of the inclusion on indices of lesser importance.

All this then over 3 months, is because the methodology illustrated applies well to medium but also fairly short periods. Finally, look at the degree of correlation of the security in question with the benchmark index, comparing the relative strength of the stock to be chosen with that of the price list.

If the stock shows relative strength to the index, it means that the stock we are choosing has a trend untied from that of the reference index, which indicates that its strength is safe even in times that are not optimal in the index of quotation.

Conclusion

Thank you for making it to the end of this book. I hope it was able to provide you with all the tools you need to achieve your financial goals.

The next step is to get started with what you have learned during the course of this book. Remember, always start with a demo account: become a profitable trader before putting your money on the table.

I hope that you find these lessons valuable and that you got the information you were looking for. Creating a "swing trading lifestyle" that works for you will give you an incredible feeling, especially at the beginning, when you make the first gains. I am thrilled for you to start and I cannot wait to see your results coming in.